COMMUNION MESSAGES

COMMUNION MESSAGES

Edited by FRANK S. MEAD

FLEMING H. REVELL COMPANY

Preface

ONE OF OUR hymns speaks of "mystic sweet communion"; the words are not used in reference to the Lord's Supper, but they well might be, for there is something both mystic and sweet about this most celebrated sacrament of the church. We love it, though we seldom fully understand it—and we misunderstand it often. Emerson left the church rather than serve it; George Washington stayed away on Communion Sundays. Rank and file, however, we come and take it and find strength in it for daily living, though we still see through a glass, darkly. . . .

To some it is a miracle of body and blood and bread and wine, in which they participate every Lord's Day; to others it is a memorial to be faithfully kept on certain stated days and seasons; to some it is a ritual followed mechanically and to some it is the broad symbol of the fellowship of believers everywhere. To all, it is a mystery. Communion and the cross are allied and have this in common: they hold power and secrets spiritual never completely revealed.

The mystery holds for the clergyman who must administer the Supper, no matter how perfectly wrought out his theology—and upon him rests the responsibility of making clear to the questing layman the meaning and the beauty and the joy of the priceless ordinance inaugurated in Jerusalem's Upper Room. How often the minister longs for a window to open, that those who take bread and cup from him may have more light and deeper understanding. . . .

This is a book of windows for the concerned clergyman . . . for him to whom repetition and the stereotyped are the eighth and ninth deadly sins. They are windows offered

5

not as escape from homiletic toil, nor yet as loot for the plagiarist, but as high moments of inspiration in the celebration of the Supper. They are windows thrown open by some of the finest minds in the church. They are windows opened toward the East and Jerusalem . . . in the prayerful hope that His presence may become clearer as we come to His Table and make new covenant with Him.

Frank S. Mead
Editor

Contents

COMMUNION MESSAGES

CHARLES L. ALLEN

BORN NEWTON COUNTY, Georgia, June 24, 1913. A.B., Wofford College, 1935; B.D., Emory University, 1937; D.D., Piedmont College, 1946; D.D., Emory University, 1960. Ordained Methodist minister, 1933. Served as pastor in Georgia for twenty-seven years, 1948-1960 at Grace Methodist Church in Atlanta. Now pastor of First Methodist Church, Houston, Texas. Columnist for Atlanta *Constitution* and other newspapers; frequently heard on radio and TV. Author, *All Things Are Possible Through Prayer; God's Psychiatry; The Touch of the Master's Hand; When the Heart Is Hungry; In Quest of God's Power; Roads to Radiant Living; When You Lose a Loved One;* co-author of *Candle, Star and Christmas Tree; Christmas in Our Hearts.*

What the Cross Means to Me

THERE IS A moving Negro spiritual which asks, "Were you there when they crucified my Lord?" That question doesn't seem strange to us. Suppose, however, it were asked concerning Socrates? "Were you there when Socrates drank the hemlock?" Of course you weren't there. That happened long before you were born.

But when you think of Calvary, it doesn't seem strange to think of yourself as being there. When Rembrandt painted the crucifixion, he showed part of the crowd. Study the faces in that crowd and you will find that one of them is Rembrandt himself. The great artist thought of himself as being there. So do we. In a deep sense, we are there. The cross is not something in the dim, distant past. We know we are part of what happened that day.

As I stand before the cross, instead of trying to explain it, I feel as though I would just like to kneel before it in reverence and humility. I know something happened that day that is different from anything that has ever happened before or since. It belongs equally to every age. The hymn-writer said, "In the cross of Christ I glory, towering o'er the wrecks of time." Somehow we instinctively know that no matter what happens, the cross will stand secure and unshaken.

When I was a little boy, I recall vividly a picture on a calendar that we kept hanging on the wall long after it

11

was out-of-date. It showed a stormy sea. The sky was overcast, lightning flashed, rain poured down. Rising above the savagely beating waves was a white towering cross. In the water below was a desperate creature reaching out. Underneath were printed the words: "Simply to Thy Cross I cling." We can't explain it—we can and do cling to it through faith.

As I look at the cross, the first truth I see there is the fact that there are some things worse than death. Betrayal is worse than death. I see Jesus in Gethsemane. He doesn't want to die—a young man of thirty-three years. There is so much more He wants to do in life. He could have saved Himself by becoming a coward or by compromising His principles. But to betray His faith, His standards, His ideals would for Him have been worse than death. That same night Judas became a betrayer. He gained some money, he saved his skin, but later he found he made a bad bargain. There are many people today who have learned what Judas learned. They would gladly swap what they have gained for a clear conscience. It is far better to let one's body die than to let the soul die.

As I see the cross, I know life is a matter of quality instead of quantity. How long a person lives is not the most important thing about life. How much a person possesses, the honors and comforts he gains, the security he attains—none of those are important enough to give our souls for.

The cross forever rebukes and destroys the proposition that the body is man's supreme possession. Jesus Himself said, "Fear not them which kill the body, but are not able to kill the soul . . ." (Matthew 10:28). There is something to live for that is more important than the body. The cross rebukes my self-centeredness.

As we stand by the cross of Christ, we see history's most complete revelation of the love of God. Leslie Weatherhead tells of being on board a ship one dark night in the Mediterranean. They were passing Stromboli, the famous island volcano. Suddenly there was a great burst of flame, lighting up the ocean for miles around. The darkness gave way to the flame of fire and then gradually the volcano subsided until it was again dark. What did it mean? It meant that for a few hours there had been revealed the fire that is continually burning in the heart of that mountain.

That is a fine illustration of the cross. As we see Jesus there, think of His reasons for being there, recognize His dying to save lost humanity, see His spirit of redemptive forgiveness toward even those who put Him there, we realize that the cross is a window through which we can see into the heart of God. The cross reveals God's love toward each of us.

> I sometimes think about the cross
> And shut my eyes, and try to see
> The cruel nails and crown of thorns,
> And Jesus, crucified for me.
> But even could I see Him die,
> I could but see a little part
> Of that great love which, like a fire,
> Is always burning in His heart.

In his book *The Meaning of the Cross* Dr. Maltby tells of a father who had a reprobate son. Again and again that father got his son out of trouble until finally the father felt forced to give up. He said, "I have had to wash my hands of him. What else could I do?" Well, whatever the complete opposite of "washing our hands" of one is, God did it on the cross.

The cross does not change God, it does not pay God off, but rather does it reveal His eternal attitude toward every man. John Donne, the seventeenth-century English preacher, pointed out that the best way to think of God's love is by thinking of a circle. He said, "A circle is endless; whom God loves, He loves to the end; and not only to their own end, to their death, but to His end." And we know that God is endless. Because God is what He is, I realize I am in the hands of a love that will never let me go. Neither will His love let me off. I may go on sinning, I may do cowardly and disappointing things, I may be less than my best, I may turn my back on His face, but God never "washes His hands of me." Like the shepherd, He seeks His lost sheep and keeps on seeking until He finds it.

Men hide from God, they refuse to face up to His claims upon their lives, they go on living day by day as if there were no God. But remember—the cross is not some incident of ancient history, it is an ever-present experience overshadowing the life of every man. It is eternal proof that God is after us. When any one of us looks honestly and clearly at the cross, we kneel before it in adoration and surrender.

One of the problems today in atomic research is the disposal of atomic waste products. Once this strange power is created, it cannot be destroyed. It cannot be burned or thrown away; even the waste of the atomic plants remains active and dangerous for thousands of years.

One day Calvary became a power plant—the power of God's eternal love was, in a very special way, released there that day. And from that day until this very moment, its power has been flowing into the lives of men. Men have run from it, fought it, belittled it, ignored it, but the power of the cross has not been diminished.

As Jesus was hanging on Calvary, He looked into the face of God and said, "It is finished" (John 19:30). What was finished? His life? No. He meant that God had sent Him to earth for a particular and special purpose. Now, on the cross, that purpose was accomplished. Something was accomplished that day that had never been accomplished before and would never need to be done again—something once and for all time.

Some mighty deed was accomplished on the cross. What that deed was none of us can answer completely, for it was in a higher realm than the natural man: it was in the realm of the supernatural. In some way that is beyond our limited understanding, our own sins—my sins, your sins—were dealt with on the cross. The salvation of the human soul, the forgiveness of sins is connected in some peculiar way to the cross of Christ. St. Paul said well: "Therefore if any man be in Christ, he is a new creature: old things are passed away; behold, all things are become new. And all things are of God, who hath reconciled us to himself by Jesus Christ. . . . To wit, that God was in Christ, reconciling the world unto himself, not imputing their trespasses unto them; and hath committed unto us the word of reconciliation" (II Corinthians 5:17-19).

On the cross the door was opened between man and God. In some way beyond our understanding, the cross made a difference in man's relationship to God. In some way, my sins were dealt with that day, and when I accept Christ as my Saviour, my sins no longer stand between my soul and God. I do not need to understand it—I need only to believe and by faith to accept it. Why was the cross necessary? The reason I cannot answer that is because my little mind is incapable of understanding the nature of God and the supernatural universe. The fact that Jesus died on the cross is proof that it was necessary—and thus I know it is necessary for me by faith to claim the cross and believe in it.

We remember Christian in *Pilgrim's Progess*, struggling along with a heavy burden. Finally he came to Calvary, climbed that hill and knelt before the cross. Then, and not until then, his burden rolled away and he became free of it and could continue his journey toward the City of God. I do not need to understand it. I only need to kneel before it. Millions can sing today, "At the cross, where I first saw the light; and the burden of my heart rolled away. . . ." May it be so for each of us.

GLENN HACKNEY ASQUITH

BORN KNOXVILLE, Tennessee, October 21, 1904; A.B., Eastern
Baptist College; Th.B., Eastern Baptist Theological Seminary;
D.D., Eastern Baptist Seminary, 1952; eighteen years in the
pastoral ministry in Baptist churches in Pennsylvania, New
Jersey, Rhode Island, Connecticut and Massachusetts. Execu-
tive secretary, New York State Baptist Convention, 1950-1956;
Executive secretary, Philadelphia Baptist Association, 1960;
editor, *Baptist New Yorker*, 1950-1956; author 1200 manu-
scripts, including two books: *Church Officers at Work; Lively
May I Walk*; included in four anthologies including Maus'
The Church and the Fine Arts; recipient of a Freedoms
Foundation Award; delegate, Baptist World Alliance, London,
1955; author of the widely quoted and reprinted leaflet, "The
Church Needs No Money."

The Call of Christ

She [Martha] went her way, and called Mary her sister se-cretly, saying, The Master is come, and calleth for thee

(JOHN 11:28).

OVER OUR HEADS is the church bell in its tower. Not too many years ago the bell rang out the call to worship, summoning men and women and boys and girls to divine worship. But it rings no longer; the tower is too weak to stand the shock of the hundreds of pounds of metal swinging back and forth. It may be that we have the same feeling concerning our Lord. It may be that we admit that He called Andrew and Peter and Matthew and the rest, yes, even so recently as our grandfathers' day He may have made His voice heard—but He calls no more; the world is so weakened by sin and age that it could not stand the sounds of the Son of Man crying out, "Come unto me all ye that are heavy-laden and I will give you rest."

There may be another explanation why we do not hear the Master's voice in our time. Scientists tell us that there can be no sound where there is no ear—either human or mechanical—to hear it. On the uninhabited desert, they say, a meteor falling to the ground would fall silently, a jet plane breaking the sound barrier would not disturb the lonely stillness. Perhaps the Christ is calling as urgently and as continuously as He did when He was here on earth, but the ears of our spirits are not open to hear Him. It may help us to be awake to His voice if we look at the when, the how, and the what of the call of Christ.

When does He call?

As it was with Mary, He calls while we are sitting in the house. Every one of us has found some sort of security for himself, some four walls of something, some roof. The instinct is with us from childhood when the little boys said, "Let's build a cabin," or when the little girls said to one another, "Let's play house." The cabins we built and the houses contrived were flimsy, but expressive of the urge to be protected. When the call came to Matthew he was sitting at the receipt of taxes, feeling secure in his house of money-making. When the call came to Peter and John they were safe in their house of business, catching and marketing fish. When the call came to Mary Magdalene she was in the house of sin. When the call came to the men in the parable one was in the house of his ancestors (he had to wait and bury his father), another was in the house of husbandry (he had to try some new oxen), a third was in the house of matrimony (he had just married)—they would not heed the call.

In Syracuse, the University bought some land for a new dormitory. One house stood in the way and the owner refused to sell at any price. Her reason was that she had always lived there and she could not face a change at her age. So the dormitory was built around her place.

No matter when the call comes we shall be found engaged and occupied, feeling secure in some house of work, of pleasure, of traditional living, and it will be difficult to get us out even to answer God. You will remember that God could not use Abram in the house in Ur, but He called him to "get up, and get out." The call is bound to shake us loose from something unworthy, if not actually evil.

And the call will come while we are mourning some loss. Mary was grieving for the dead brother, Lazarus. Like the turtle who withdraws into his shell at the first sign of danger, she had withdrawn from the world because she had been hurt.

I suppose that none of us here but has some dead hope, some dead ambition, some dead love; I suppose that none of us but is grieving over some loss. The virtue we had but have no longer, the opportunity which knocked and found us unresponsive, the friends who failed us, the dreams which burst like bubbles and left us bitter, the great plans which we were not brave enough to carry through—these are the things which grieve us. And at such a time the call of Christ comes. Then our Lord says, "Let the dead bury their own dead—come and follow me." Memory cannot be erased, but we can somehow be withdrawn from the scene of death. When we reach maturity, it sometimes seems as though the events of our childhood may have happened to someone else. So it is with the call of Christ to us—we can be changed until the dead things of the past are quite remote. After Paul had become the prisoner of Jesus Christ, it must have been hard for him to recognize himself as the young man with hatred in his heart who held the coats of those who stoned Stephen.

Further, the call comes while others are working and we are withdrawn from the service of God and man. Martha was outside to greet her Lord, she was engaging in the daily tasks, but Mary permitted herself to be overwhelmed by the great tragedy in the family. When I was called to denominational work, I felt that the whole state program had been waiting for me because of the enthusiasm I felt for the new task, but I quickly found that scores of other men had been called and the work had received their time, their sacrifices, and their love. When the call comes to any individual, he must realize that millions of others have heard the Christ before and that he is being highly honored to join the great company of the redeemed. Until the call is heard and heeded you and I are outside in the cold streets of the world while others are inside the Kingdom in the warmth of God's forgiveness and grace.

As to how the call comes, we know that it comes through some other person in the majority of cases. Martha came to tell Mary that the Master was calling her, Andrew went to tell Peter, the Samaritan woman went back to tell her whole city, priests, prophets and preachers have been telling others throughout the generations; and we are hoping to get through to someone here today with the message that the crucified and risen Saviour is urgently calling that one. When a wealthy person dies, the executor of the estate leaves nothing undone to discover all of the heirs under the will, and to tell each one that he is a beneficiary. Every one of us who has been called by the Lord is an executor of the estate and each of us has the obligation to hunt some other heir under the will, and to say, "You are called to enter into your inheritance."

A man was bitten by a dog and the dog was discovered to have rabies. But the man had disappeared and no one knew who he was—some children had seen a strange man attacked by the dog, but they did not know him and could not help in identifying him. Then followed one of those real-life dramas that is far more exciting than fiction. Pleas went out over the radio for the man to get to the nearest hospital or police station, and the local newspapers put the warning on the front page in great black letters, every doctor and every hospital in town was put on the alert in the event that a man should come for treatment. The hours passed and the time for preventive treatment was running out. Where was the man? How to save him from certain death? Happily he heard the radio news just in time and hastened to get treatment. But—if no effort had been made, if the officials and citizens had left it up to chance or the man's good judgment, he could have died in agony. Is it not so with us who have heard the call of Christ? There is a remedy for sinful men, but time runs out as human life is spent. This cannot be left to chance or to the inner urgings of the infected soul—the call must come through some servant of God.

Usually the call comes secretly. Without announcing what she was doing, Martha went secretly into the house to tell Mary. As I talk to you, I cannot tell to which of you the Lord may be speaking urgently. It is as Jesus said to Nicodemus, that the wind blows here and there without anyone knowing whence it came or whither it goes, and that it is true with everyone to whom the Spirit speaks. No matter how loudly the messenger cries the word, it will be the still, small voice within which will confirm the call. The records of flight are filled with instance of tower-control men doing their best to get in touch with planes flying in perilous weather and not knowing whether or not the instructions are heard. The pilot must have a workable receiving set and have it turned on, or he does not hear. The messages go through the air silently, and must be accepted by the man at the other end. We know in our own homes that the air is filled with impulses which will bring sound and pictures into the TV set, but the set must be in good order and the power must be turned on. I am sure that God is speaking to each of us at this moment—but how many, in the secrecy of their hearts and souls, are listening to the words?

Another thing which we need to know is that the call comes through people only by the instruction of God. Martha had been told by Jesus that He would speak to Mary. In our day we have a terrible spirit of independence which resents the intervention of some third party. In one of my churches the adjoining buildings were not more than ten feet away. It seemed a firetrap to me and I inquired as to insurance. But I was told: "There have been buildings burned on each side of us, but the church is still here—if God wants to burn the church He will, but apparently He does not want to." They resented the intrusion of the insurance man—they were going to deal with God directly. With most of us, however, we must accept the authority of the one who brings the message, for God has instructed him to give it to us. Even though the Apostle Paul had a direct vision of God, he went in his blindness until God sent Ananias to touch him and teach him. If you have heard the call, you may be able to think at this minute who it was that God had sent to you with the message—a pastor, a teacher, a parent, a friend.

But what does the call do when it is heard?

First, it brings action and haste. Mary rose up quickly to find her Lord. When a baby cries in the night, the father may say, "Oh, let him cry—probably just a bad dream," but the mother gets up quickly and rushes to the child. When he calls she must answer. The cry of "Fire" in a building brings everyone out running. Believe me, the call of the Christ is no less urgent. You may hear it now, but if you neglect it now, the world and the cares of life may prevent your ever hearing it again. At the edge of western deserts the last automobile service station and restaurant will advertise in large letters, "Last chance to make sure you have enough water and gas and food until you get to the other side." A careless motorist who laughs at the sign as a clever way to get business may break down halfway across and may die before help comes. The call of God is a precious and an urgent thing demanding action and haste.

The call will provide nearness to God. Mary rose up and went out and found herself in the very presence of her Lord. Perhaps we underestimate the value of this. Think of a mountain climber with a guide. The amateur must keep close to the guide, must watch so he can put his feet in the same safe spots tested by the guide, must be close enough to see which turn to take and which soft places to avoid. So with us as we journey through life: we are not safe unless we stay close to our Master. In the parable of the hundred sheep and the shepherd, ninety-nine stayed close to the shepherd but one drifted away. In the parable the keeper of the sheep found the one-hundredth sheep, but in real life the average shepherd would fail to find the animal alive. When the shepherd calls us and we follow the voice we shall be gathered safely into the eternal fold. Oh, how much it means to us in time of trouble, despair, bereavement, or failure to know that we are very close to God who knows all, can do all things, who loves us with an everlasting love!

Last of all, the call restores our dead hopes. We mourn until we hear the voice of God, and then we rejoice.

Perhaps we have given ourselves up as failures and then the call comes. What new energy and will is born within us to do the thing which we thought ourselves unable to do. A woman who had had a series of misfortunes settled down to a routine life of obscurity. Then she read something which told her that she had untold possibilities. Within a year she had published two books and many articles, and had become a sought-after lecturer. She needed just one spark, and that came to her. If a printed word can do this, how much more the call of God!

We may have given ourselves up because of some sin committed. We may have felt forever lost to good living and decency. Mary Magdalene thought so too, but when Jesus spoke to her she became a new person—so much so that she figures largely in the resurrection story. You and I too can give up the old ways and be born again.

Or, we may have come to the point where we have seen the years creep on and our best work done until, as one expressed it, "the future is behind us" so far as we are concerned. And then the call of the Christ shows us that the best is yet to be, that we have not started to live and achieve.

Just think of Mary in the house, surrounded by ten professional mourners, with her face veiled, clothed in yards and yards of dismal garments, with ashes strewn about, with the traditional wailing for the dead bringing tears to her eyes. It never entered her head that Lazarus could ever be anything but dead—until the Lord called her. And then she knew that He could do whatever He would; she heard Him say, "I am the resurrection and the life." I am confident that that means the raising of the person within me and you who has been dead in trespasses and sins; I am sure that it means the revival of every worthy hope and ambition and joy which have been taken from us.

We cannot possibly know what it meant to Mary, sitting there in the darkened house surrounded by mourning and mourners, with her heart leaden within her, when Martha came quietly to say, "The Master is here and calleth for thee."

But you and I can know what it means now. There is no one here who has come to church without a worry or a woe. We can know the joy of hearing at this moment and in our day, "The Master is here, and calls for *you*." He is not calling for a better person or a more useful person— He is calling for *you*. Does the call come through, or will it dissipate itself on the desert air of your own unbelief or unwillingness? Will you go out content to mourn forever, or will you go out with the best that is within you brought back to glorious life?

"Behold, I stand at the door, and knock: if any man hear my voice, and open the door, I will come in. . . ."

ANDREW W. BLACKWOOD

BORN CLAY CENTER, Kansas, August 5, 1882. A.B., Franklin College, 1902; A.B., *magna cum laude,* Harvard, 1905; student Princeton Theological Seminary, 1905-1906, Xenia Theological Seminary, 1906-1908; D.D., University of South Carolina, 1918. Ordained United Presbyterian Church, 1908. Pastor: Sixth United Presbyterian Church, Pittsburgh, Pennsylvania; First Presbyterian Church, Columbia, South Carolina; Indianola Church, Columbus, Ohio. Professor: English Bible, Presbyterian Theological Seminary, Louisville, Kentucky; Homiletics, Princeton Theological Seminary, Princeton, New Jersey; Preaching, School of Theology, Temple University, Philadelphia, Pennsylvania. Author, *The Fine Art of Preaching; The Fine Art of Public Worship; The Funeral; The Preparation of Sermons; Pastoral Leadership; Planning a Year's Pulpit Work; Leading in Public Prayer; The Growing Minister;* and many other books.

The Lord's Supper as a Sermon

As often as you eat this bread and drink the cup, you proclaim the Lord's death until he comes (I CORINTHIANS 11:26, RSV).

CHRISTIAN FRIENDS, as we draw near to "the Holy Communion of the body and blood of Jesus Christ," let us reverently think about the Lord's Supper as a sermon in action. In the Greek New Testament the central verb of our text appears seventeen times. In all these cases except two the term means to "proclaim," or to "preach." And so the word may mean here: "As often as you eat this bread and drink this cup, you preach." Who preaches? You, dear friends, as a congregation of God's redeemed children. What a privilege! What an honor!

The Sermon in the Supper is worthy of note for simplicity. It appeals mainly to the eye of the soul, but also to the other senses that bring the facts of God straight to the heart. More than almost any other message on earth, this sermon has to do only with Christ, and with us as we draw near to Him in holy love and adoration. In pointing every eye to Him as our Redeemer, and in moving every heart to receive Him anew, the Sermon in the Supper centers round the most important thing that our Redeemer ever did on earth, the one thing that He came from heaven to do "for us men and for our salvation." That one thing was to die.

29

So let us look at the Lord Jesus Christ, high and lifted up in the Lord's Supper, as the supreme sermon on earth. Here He stands forth in three different aspects, all of which have to do with time, as well as eternity.

By faith, looking back to Calvary, we behold in the Supper *the Christ of yesterday* as the Christ of the cross. In the New Testament almost every important passage about the institution of the communion relates it directly to the cross. So it seems that the first main purpose of the Sermon in the Supper is to remind us mortals that the Saviour suffered there to set us free from sin, and that He did not die in vain. To make this truth so clear and so strong that we can never forget, the Lord Jesus Himself employed two sacramental symbols.

The bread, as everyone knows, represents the body of the Lord Jesus. The breaking of the bread, a vital part of the sermon in action, reminds us repeatedly of the death that came to His dear body. In like manner the cup of blessing represents the life of our Redeemer, the life that He poured out on Calvary. This He chose to do and this He did, once and forever, to set us free from the guilt and the shame of sin. Thus He prepares us to become members of His church, the family of God's redeemed children, both on earth and in heaven.

The eating and drinking together also has a holy meaning. Drawn together by our faith in Him and our love for Him, we show our loyalty to Him by sitting together at His Table. There we meditate most of all upon the love divine that would not let us mortals go on in paths of sin and shame, the love that held not back from the cross, the love that most fully and wondrously reveals the heart of God the heavenly Father. On the other hand, the

Apostle here exhorts us to examine ourselves, one by one, lest we overlook the meaning and the spiritual value of the communion feast. Paul says, most solemnly, that if in the sacrament we do not discern the Lord's body on the cross, we may eat and drink to ourselves the condemnation of the holy God.

We ought also to examine the hymns that we sing as inseparable parts of the Holy Communion. Of course, no intelligent Christian would select for this high purpose a sweet Chautauqua song, "Break Thou the Bread of Life," a pleasing prayer that has to do with the Sea of Galilee, not with the Mount of Calvary. In the standard hymnal of a certain major denomination, the editors list eleven songs for Holy Communion. Of the eleven, only three sing much about the death of Christ, and not one of the eleven ranks among the supreme hymns in any standard book of praise.

What are the supreme hymns of Christendom? Some years ago a student of hymnology made an exhaustive study of the hymns most loved and used in the churches of Christendom. At the top of the list he put twelve hymns, six of them mainly about the death of our Redeemer. Among the twelve, the first, the second, the third, the fifth, the ninth, and the twelfth all had to do mainly with the cross.

Why do these six hymns, including the three most beloved of all, sing about the cross? Because the writers had learned from Isaiah 53, John 3:16, and countless other Bible passages, the supremacy of the cross. Why then do many of us today sing about something else in the heart of the Holy Communion? Perhaps because we are more intent upon ourselves and our feelings than upon the Saviour and His dying love. Or it may be that we hesitate to sing much about the sins and the death from which He has set us free. If so, let me ask where else on earth we can find a better sacramental song than the one that many of us consider the noblest of all our hymns, "When I Survey the Wondrous Cross"?

The Sermon in the Supper likewise bids all of us believers see in *the Christ of today* the Lord of His church. Where is the Lord Jesus, who once died and for a while lay buried? He is in glory at the right hand of God. But by His Spirit He is likewise here with us in His church. This may well be the most important fact about Him, between the close of His earthly mission and the end of the present age. This fact about the living Christ ought to dominate the observance of the communion feast. According to John Calvin, when Christ says to believers today, "This is my body," He means that this symbolic act presents the body of Christ. For many such reasons we Protestants rejoice to believe in the Real Presence of Christ in the sacrament.

As we sit together in heavenly places we ought to think much about the Christ of today, the Christ of Christian experience, the Christ of the holy Christian Church. He is here. He knows all about us, and still He loves us. Once He died for us. Now He lives with us. By His Spirit He dwells in us who believe. He cares. How much He cares! In all our afflictions He is afflicted. In all our joys He rejoices. He is able, and waiting, to do for the redeemed children of God what no one else on earth can even attempt to do.

As we commune with Him, much of the time in holy silence, He wishes us to have Christian fellowship with one another. He wishes our hearts also to go out, as His own heart ever goes out, to the whole family of God on earth and in heaven. Hence we ought lovingly to commune with the loved ones about us in the sanctuary; with the loved ones beyond the seven seas, far away from us in miles, but ever near to the heart of God; and with saints of God whom we have never seen; above all, saints who suffer in lands where Christ does not yet have His way.

Not least does our Lord wish our hearts to commune with "the spirits of just men [and women] made perfect." According to a foremost Bible scholar, in the New Testament the center of gravity lies beyond the grave. He means in part that our belief in the "communion of saints" ought ever to embrace those who have heard the trumpet calling them home, saints who have crossed the river that men call death so as to enter into the City of God, to us unseen save by the eyes of faith as we commune with them in the holy silence of the sacrament.

All of this has to do with the blessed fact of the living Christ. At the communion, as elsewhere, we who believe ought to think of Him as with us now, tender to sympathize, mighty to save, and waiting to bless. All of this emphasis on communing with the Christ of today agrees with the teachings of the New Testament. Among eight pivotal statements there about the meaning of the Lord's Supper, only one has to do with our remembrance of the past, and only one with our hope for the future. The other six all relate to communing with Him and with His beloved, here and now.

Often at the sacrament we seem to forget that He who once died is alive forevermore, and that by His Spirit, Christ is here. In Jerusalem one morning at five o'clock a small company of us gathered in a subterranean part of the Church of the Holy Sepulchre. There the Roman Catholics and others believe that the body of Christ lay on a certain slab between Good Friday and Easter morning. Down on our knees for twenty minutes we waited while a leader of would-be worship led in Latin recollections of the dead Redeemer. Then at last I staggered up the steps and out into the sunlight streaming over the summit of Mount Scopus. Down in that lower room I had felt disconsolately: "They have taken away my Lord, and I know not where they have laid Him." But in that morning light, with its "air of increased visibility," my heart leaped up as I exclaimed: "Lo, Christ is here! He lives! He lives!"

So at the Holy Communion, when we "preach the Lord's death," let us do so with joy because by His Spirit the Lord Jesus is ever with us, and never so clearly as at His Table. All the while, as James Denney wrote in *Studies in Theology:* "The Church lives, not [only] by what Christ was, but [also] by what He is; not only by what He did, but supremely because of what He does. . . . When we preach from the Gospels, and see what Jesus was, and said, and did, and suffered, let us remember to make the application in the present tense. . . . Faith always has its object here and now, and without faith there is no [Christian] religion."

In the Lord's Supper as a sermon, *the Christ of tomorrow* stands out as the King with His crown. At Holy Communion we ought to make much of what the Scottish fathers called "the crown rights of our Redeemer." "The Head that once was crowned with thorns is crowned with glory now." In the best all-round congregation that I have ever known well, this was perhaps the favorite hymn, the one that the people sang with holy abandon like that of heaven. And why? Because in the sacrament and elsewhere they had learned to think in terms of our text, not least about the words at the close: "As often as you eat this bread and drink the cup, you [preach] the Lord's death until he comes."

"Until He comes!" These climactic words point to the final return of our Lord. Much as we Christians rejoice in the first advent at Christmas, we ought even more to rejoice in His final advent. Clearly and wondrously as the Scriptures reveal His first appearing to save us mortals from our sins, much more fully and wondrously does the written Word of God reveal the certainty and the glory of His final appearing, when He shall take to Himself the crown that He died to win as King of earth as well as heaven. However much we ignore the fact, this blessed hope provides the climactic truth about the Lord's Supper as a sermon. In the sacrament you are to show the Lord's death until He comes in glory as the King of kings.

At the communion table we Christians preach the truth about the end of the present age. Then no longer shall we witness "truth forever on the scaffold; wrong forever on the throne." At the time of our Lord's appearing, the kingdoms of this old sin-cursed, war-weary, sorrow-stricken world shall become the Kingdom of our Lord and of His Christ, the Kingdom that is righteousness, peace, and joy in the Holy Spirit. Wherefore, Christian friends, lift up your hearts. Lift them up unto the Lord.

The final advent of our Lord will mark the beginning of the eternal age. Then, and only then, shall we witness the fulfillment of all our rosy dreams, and the consummation of all our worthy hopes, hopes that are "fixed on Jesus' blood and righteousness." If at times we wonder why in the church of today many of us have lost the luster and the radiance of believers in apostolic times, one reason may be that even at the communion table we do not rest our hopes on triumphant assurance of Christ's coming in glory at the end of this awful age.

In that congregation to which I have already referred, custom decreed that on Communion Day there be no sermon and no spoken words of meditation. After a period of uplifting worship, with hymns and Scripture readings and prayers, came the Holy Sacrament. In a church that strongly stressed the preaching of the Word, the brethren on that day felt no need of a sermon other than the one in the Lord's Supper. On that high day of the feast, as on other days of rest and worship, the balcony on either side would be filled with students. But, unlike most other days, after the hour of worship had come to an end, one or more of those university students would find the way to the front of the church and there make known a desire to confess faith in Christ, and thus be received into the fellowship of the Christian Church.

In a congregation that celebrated the Lord's Supper too seldom—statedly only once a quarter—why did more young university men profess their faith in Christ after the communion service than after all the intervening sermons? Because they saw and felt in that one hour of worship the mystery and the wonder of the Triune God, as that mystery and wonder come to us mortals through the Lord's Supper as the supreme Christian sermon on earth. At the Table of the Lord, even more than at any other place here below, He stands ready to fulfill His ever-present promise: "I, if I be lifted up from the earth, will draw all men unto me" (John 12:32). Literally, this means "to be lifted up out of the earth." Today, through the Holy Communion as a sermon, the uplifted Christ is drawing us to Himself as our Redeemer and our King.

Christian friend, as you draw near to the Holy Communion, the Lord Jesus is bestowing on you an honor that even an angel might well desire. The Lord Christ is bidding you take part in preaching the Sermon in the Supper. Before you accept His gracious invitation, He wishes you to dedicate yourself anew to Him and to His Kingdom. If by faith you so dedicate yourself, and worthily take your part in preaching the Sermon in the Supper, He will bless you with the riches of His grace. Only by His favor can any of us sinners ever prove worthy to enter into the Holy Communion as earth's nearest approach to heaven. So to His glory now join with me in an ascription of praise:

Glory be to Thee, O God, for the grace that appeared at the first advent of our Lord, for the redeeming power of His cross, and for the hope of heaven. Glory be to Thee, O Christ, for Thy death upon the cross, for Thy presence in our communion feast, and for the assurance of Thy final advent. Glory be to Thee, O Spirit of God, for opening our eyes that we may behold the glory of the Lord Jesus, for opening our hearts to receive Him as Redeemer, and for opening the way for us to preach the Sermon in the Lord's Supper. Glory be to the Triune God for the wonders of redemption in the past, the wonders of Christian experience in the present, and the wonders of Christian hope for all time to come—wonders that we are soon to preach through the Sermon in the Supper.

EDWARD L. R. ELSON

BORN MONONGAHELA, PENNSYLVANIA, December 23, 1906; A.B., Asbury College, 1928; M.Th., University of Southern California, 1931; honorary doctorates bestowed by fifteen American colleges and universities. Ordained at Santa Monica, California, April, 1930, by the Presbytery of Los Angeles. Pastor, First Presbyterian Church, La Jolla, California, 1931-1941; pastor, The National Presbyterian Church, Washington, D.C., since 1946. Commissioned Chaplain, U. S. Army Reserve, 1930. Active duty 1941-1946. Received numerous high decorations from the United States and foreign governments; president of the Washington Council of Churches for two terms; member of Board of Trustees, Wilson College and Maryville College; chairman, National Council, American Friends of the Middle East; named "Churchman of the Year," 1954; frequent speaker at colleges and universities. Author, *One Moment with God, America's Spiritual Recovery, And Still He Speaks,* and feature articles in church and secular journals.

Guests at the Lord's Table

When the hour came, he sat at table, and the apostles with him (LUKE 22:14, RSV).

TWELVE MEN sat down with our Lord at the first communion service. They represented the whole of mankind. They were real men, not angels. The title "Saint" had not been prefixed to their names. They earned that appellation by their perseverance as the "redeemed of the Lord" and by their fidelity to His great commission. They were men of the people and of the great out-of-doors. Their talents were varied and sufficient. The Master was sure they would understand the people and be understood by them. Some of them were rough fellows, some were more refined and polished. Some were capricious and some stormy in disposition; others were men of quiet demeanor and consistent sound judgment. When they set out to follow Jesus, they followed Him with their own temperaments and personalities. They were not deprived of their individuality; each man was an unduplicated entity. Each man had his own fellowship with the Master. When He sent them out they went out in the power of their own manhood.

"The names of the twelve apostles are these: first, Simon, who is called Peter, and Andrew his brother; James the son of Zebedee, and John his brother; Philip and Bartholomew;

Thomas and Matthew the tax collector; James the son of Alphaeus, and Thaddaeus; Simon the Cananaean, and Judas Iscariot, who betrayed him" (Matthew 10:2-4, rsv). These all sat with our Lord that night. And to every celebration of the Holy Commuion of the Lord's Supper since that night come counterparts of each original disciple.

Peter was at the table that night. He was the man of impulse. He followed Jesus with reckless enthusiasm, rushing in where "angels fear to tread." He was "quick on the draw." There was nothing timid about Peter. He elbowed his way into every situation. He was not a wallflower, avoiding participation in events. He threw himself into every action. He had the ability to size up a situation, make a decision, and act at that moment. Men could see all there was of him—his inner life was exposed to view. Sometimes he acted without sufficient reflection and evaluation, but he always acted and then accepted responsibility for his actions. When the Master called him from his fishing, he left his work and gave all he had to the new enterprise.

One night Peter fished with the apostles and in the early dawn saw Jesus standing on the shore. The Master called out across the lake, "Have you any fish?" The disciples were mystified and speculative. Peter exclaimed, "It is the Lord!" Not satisfied with long distance communications he leaped overboard and swam ashore to greet his Master.

One day there was a debate about the identity of Jesus. The Master asked what men were saying about Him, who He was. Then He turned to His Apostles and asked, "But who do you say that I am?" Peter was first to respond. Peter knew. Peter exclaimed, "You are the Christ, the Son of the living God."

On that night of sacred memory when Jesus took the towel and went about from man to man washing the feet of the apostles, Peter was agitated at the thought of his Lord washing his feet. "You shall never wash my feet," Peter said. But after a word from the gentle Saviour Peter yielded not simply for the washing of his feet but for entire cleansing, "Lord, not my feet only but also my hands and my head!"

Then there came a day when Peter resolutely pledged his loyalty to Jesus, but before the dawn when the cock was beginning to herald a new day he denied his Lord—then "went out and wept bitterly."

But look at the way the Lord employed Peter. People sneered when Jesus called Simon "Petros"—the rock. They smiled and said there was not much solid substance in that fellow. But Jesus' faith in Peter made the difference. Jesus put backbone and stability into him. Jesus announced that He would build His church upon such a type of human character and temperament. Peter came through. Peter did not let his Lord down. After Calvary and Easter Day came the day of Pentecost. Then it was noted that "when the people saw the boldness of Peter and John, they took knowledge of them that they had been with Jesus."

Now Peter goes to every communion service. In every age there are those whose excessive enthusiasm and misplaced emphasis are an embarrassment to others. There are some whose generous ardor and fanatical zeal repulse rather than attract. When Jesus is having a hard time, when the church is being sorely tested, there are some who want to run away. There are some who will deny their Lord when Jesus is having a difficult time and when there is a cross to face, and then will repent with true humility, atoning for their infidelity with new acts of loyalty. In every congregation, at every communion appears the man of alternating moods—of high ardor and low loyalty. He comes and hears his blessed Lord say once again, "This is my body broken for you." Peter continues to come to the Holy Table of the Lord. Even as Peter of old was the chief apostle, so today such souls are the foundation of the church.

James was at the first communion service. Although little is recorded about James, Jesus must have valued his character and service for he belonged to the triumvirate which entered into the most intimate experiences of our Lord's life. How often we read that He took "Peter, James and John" with Him. James was with the Lord on the Mount of Transfiguration. He entered into the sorrow of the Garden of Gethsemane. In contrast with Peter, James was the modest, reserved man of quiet poise. In loyalty, without extravagant demonstration, he followed Jesus in all His varied experiences until the very end.

James, the dependable man of few words, will be at every communion service. Such persons are the strength of the church. They are those who work in silence, whose love is deep and whose loyalty is strong. They are not given to emotional outbursts. The ecstasies they allow others. Theirs is a religion of the heart, deep and undisturbed by surface currents. To the man of silence, religion is an everyday affair. Too many mar their good deeds by extravagant talk, while the Jameses in the church go about doing the work. It is a good thing to find some of James's type in the church when so often motion is mistaken for work and noise for power. How much we need the quiet dependable discipline of James. He comes to communion and hears the gracious words of the Host, "Blessed are they that hunger and thirst after righteousness for they shall be filled."

John sat at the table that night. He was a man of great strength. It seems likely that there were three Johns in the New Testament and quite as likely three different Johns in the one man who was the apostle. The real John of the Gospels was referred to as one of the "sons of thunder." He was a whirlwind of enthusiasm and a tornado of wrath. Only after grace had done its work did he become the serene Saint John.

This man was a man of violent temper. On one occasion as the disciples traveled, they entered a Samaritan village toward nightfall and sought overnight lodging. But because the Master appeared to be going toward Jerusalem, and was obviously a Jew, the Samaritans would not allow him to sleep in their town. John was so angry he wanted to burn the town down and would have liked the honor of setting the torch to it. When Jesus was insulted, this man of fierce loyalty and hot temper would destroy the offenders, and he would do it at once.

One day John observed a man going about doing good, casting out devils in Jesus' name. John yelled, "Stop it! Stop it!" and then hurried to report to his Lord. "Teacher, we saw a man casting out demons in your name, and we forbade him, because he was not following us." This man did not belong to John's sect. But Jesus rebuked His intemperate disciple, "Do not forbid him . . . he that is not against us is for us" (Mark 9:38, 39, 40, RSV).

In the early years all of the disciples looked toward the establishment of a temporal kingdom in which they would have preferment. John, with his brother James—the sons of Zebedee—approached the Master saying, "Grant unto us that we may sit, one on thy right hand, and the other on thy left hand, in thy glory." There was no reticence here, only zeal and ambition. Jesus, wanting to be sure of their qualifications, asked, "Can ye drink of the cup that I drink of?" They answered without hesitation, "We can" (Mark 10:35-39). John felt himself fit to be near Jesus. He was the right-hand man and he knew it.

God can use a man of strong purpose. The man who does not become angry at times may not have much moral strength. There are occasions when only wrath is appropriate. The holier a man becomes the more sensitive he is to evil. John was one of those persons liable to quick, hot anger. But divine grace was at work in John and he grew more like the Master with the passing of the years. He was beneath the cross at Calvary and heard the anguished Saviour, looking first at Mary and then at John, say, "Woman, behold thy son! . . . [Son] behold thy mother. And from that hour," the record says, "that disciple took her unto his own home."

Who can ever know how many like John come to communion? The hot-tempered John brings all his electric storms to the Lord. The sectarian John who disclaims others because they "follow not with us" comes to the table. It is not the man who comes to communion but the man who departs who makes the difference in the Kingdom. It is not the guest but the Host who transforms John the man into John the saint. The table is not his but the Lord's. Jesus is the Host. He bids such strong men as John to remember Him, to take, eat, and be transformed by His grace.

Matthew sat there at the table that night. What a risky

thing Jesus did that day as He passed the tax booth on the wharf and called Matthew from his books and coins to follow Him. A tax collector and a publican in the apostolic band always raised questions in the minds of the people. Matthew, huddled in his little shed, collecting "tainted money" for Rome, was loathed by his fellow countrymen. You get the depth of resentment in the prayer of the Pharisee, "God, I thank thee, that I am not as other men are, extortioners, unjust . . . or even as this publican." No person was lower in the social scale. It was not that he was a businessman. Every Jew honored a businessman. It was that this man's talents were in the service of the Imperial Government, and he was protected in his duties by occupation forces. Yet Jesus dined "with publicans and sinners." When Matthew followed Jesus he forsook his work for Rome. He turned his back upon his own lucrative profession. He became a businessman for his Lord, giving himself and all his talents to the Master's enterprise. His business ability was spiritualized and redirected. In many types Matthew sits at every communion table.

Thomas was at that communion table. People call him "Doubting Thomas." He wanted all the evidence he could get before following the resurrected Lord. Then he heard the living Christ say, "Reach hither thy hand . . . and be not faithless, but believing." Faith received its answer and he called out in one exultant shout, "My Lord and my God." A man's doubt is always the doubt of his faith. It is a good thing to ask questions, to want the most credible basis for faith. It is a good thing for a man to be inquisitive, to seek attestation and confirmation. Some men will only believe on the most convincing evidence. But once convinced they are invincible. There is a multitude in the apostolic succession of Thomas, the company of those "who have not seen, and yet have believed." This host of inquiring seekers after reality hear His gracious words uttered at the table as they were uttered long ago in the Upper Room, "Peace be unto you."

Even Judas sat with his Lord in the first communion. He was a man of high privilege. He saw the glory of the eternal in the face of Jesus Christ and listened to His matchless words. Yet he forfeited his highest destiny by betrayal, soiling forever the name of Judas. Every disciple was a venture with Jesus, but Judas was the only one who, in the greatest test, was disloyal. He was the one "who might have been." The spirit of avarice encouraged his treacherous purposes. "I have sinned," he cried, "I have betrayed innocent blood." He promptly went out and hanged himself. "And it was night." Outside and inside the man it was all black.

"And the names of the disciples are these": Peter, the impetuous; James, the silent; John, the hot-tempered; Matthew, the redeemed agent of the enemy power; Judas, the man who lost his chance; Andrew, the practical, decisive man; Philip, the matter-of-fact man; Thomas, the investigative man; Simon Zelotes, the enthusiast; James, son of Alphaeus to whom the least things were infinitely important; Lebbaeus and Bartholomew the obscure but faithful. All these men sat with the Saviour at the first communion service. So now all these types and temperaments among the people of God who call Jesus Christ Lord and Saviour surround the table where the "joy of his salvation" is restored to them. It is His table, not ours. He is the Host. We are His guests, gathered around the sacred tokens of His redemption. Here men, women, boys, and girls in all their great variety of need hear Him say, "Come unto me"; "Blessed are they which do hunger and thirst after righteousness: for they shall be filled"; "This do in remembrance of me."

A. REUBEN GORNITZKA

BORN SEATTLE, WASHINGTON, November 12, 1917. Graduate, St. Olaf College, Northfield, Minnesota, 1939; Luther Theological Seminary, St. Paul, Minnesota, 1943; additional study at Maywood Theological Seminary, Union Theological Seminary, and Wartburg Theological Seminary; D.D., Capital University, Columbus, Ohio, 1959. Ordained, 1943; associate pastor, Bethel Lutheran Church, Madison, Wisconsin; pastor, Our Savior's Lutheran Church, Milwaukee; senior pastor, Central Lutheran Church, Minneapolis, since 1955. Chairman, Urban Church Planning Committee, Evangelical Lutheran Church; member, Board of Directors, Greater Minneapolis Council of Churches; member, Board of Regents, Luther College; member, Board of Directors, YMCA; president, Minneapolis Ministerial Association.

Dr. Gornitzka, who ministers at Central Lutheran Church to more than 4,000 sanctuary worshipers and 100,000 radio listeners, has done extensive work in radio and television broadcasting and has often spoken at church conferences, Bible camps, meetings of civic organizations, commencement services, and college and university Religious Emphasis Weeks. He has traveled throughout the United States, England, the Scandinavian countries, Europe, and the Near East. A contributor to *The Lutheran Herald, The Lutheran Teacher*, and other periodicals, he is author of *Seriously Now* and *It's Your Life*.

Take a Clean Dish

*Our dear Heavenly Father, forgive our foolish ways, restore
us in a rightful mind; in purer life Thy service find, in deeper
reverence praise. Amen.*

THERE IS A bit of humor in the story of a bachelor who had
lived alone for many years in the north woods. There came
a day when he married, to the surprise of his friends who
questioned him as to why he had had this change of mind
after so many years. His explanation went something like
this: For a number of years he had lived alone, doing his
own cooking in a very simple sort of way. Becoming quite
bored with the sameness of his menus, he secured a book
of recipes and began with some effort to produce something new for his own table. He decided to marry because,
he said, "Every time I picked up the cookbook and began
to read a new recipe, it always started with the words 'take
a clean dish.' I wasn't too interested in that part of it."

Now I'd like to suggest that there are a number of areas
of life in which it is exceedingly important that you and I
know the experience of taking a clean dish, of starting
anew. It is so in the realm of the spiritual. The Apostle
Paul, in addressing himself to the Christians at Philippi,
says, "Brethren, I count not myself to have apprehended:
but this one thing I do, forgetting those things which are
behind, and reaching forth unto those things which are

49

before, I press toward the mark for the prize of the high calling of God in Christ Jesus" (Philippians 3:13, 14). This, I think, is one of the most fascinating things that Paul ever wrote. Although we could dwell upon any one of the several facets of this statement, I would like to have you think with me about the phrase, "forgetting the things which are behind."

The Apostle Paul indicates that there is something important for the individual in his spiritual life in "taking a clean dish," in starting out afresh. This is important in two directions. It can have to do with some major point in one's life experience when, having gone one way, lived one way and moved in a certain direction, there is a complete turnabout. The past is washed out and left behind—it is tomorrow, the future, that is now of importance. But this is true not only for the new believer who may have left a life apart from God and for the first time tied his life to Jesus Christ, but also for the Christian in his everyday experience. Yesterday must be left behind. With the beginnings of this day and with the new dawning of the sun, there must be a taking of a clean dish, a beginning afresh, a starting anew.

Now I think that we have very little difficulty in recognizing the importance of "forgetting the things that are behind," of "taking a clean dish," in our workaday lives. I think, for example, of a man who is a machinist. He stands in a shop and works with an expensive machine, tooling some very expensive metal. Yesterday, as he stood at that machine, an error was made. It may have been his own, or perhaps there was a defect in the metal. At any rate, an expensive piece that was being tooled was ruined. Suppose that this morning he were to concentrate on yesterday's failure. The very concentration upon that fact would suggest the possibility of another failure today.

Perhaps some of you may remember a year in your student days when you did very poor work. You did not concentrate your efforts. You did not give the time you should have, or center your attention as you ought upon the responsibilities that were yours as a student in the classroom. The results were not very good. If, in the following year, you concentrated your attention and your thought in remembering what had happened the year before, rather than recognizing that with concerted effort you could do well in this new year, no success would result. But if you were to recognize in this new day an opportunity for new knowledge, for a new concentration, for a better use of ability and time, then what transpired might be highly successful and very gratifying.

Every last one of us knows the meaning of failure in different areas of life. This may revolve about an experience in one's work, in one's association and relationships with others, in one's own personal seeking after development and growth, and not least, within one's spiritual experience and relationship to God. "Forgetting the things which are behind" meant something of real importance to the Apostle Paul. He thought about his own relationship to God, to himself and to his fellow men.

There are, I believe, two particular directions in which the Apostle Paul may have been thinking when he penned these words. It may seem that these two thoughts are diametrically opposed, yet they contain some important parallels. Perhaps Paul had first in mind, as he wrote about "forgetting the things that are behind," the experiences in the past which had been the "successes" of his spiritual life. He could be happy about these things and grateful to God. Yet he was acutely aware that he could not dwell on them indefinitely or live by these alone in the future.

We remember that remarkable experience of Paul's on the Damascus Road when he came to know for the first time what it meant for Christ to be his Lord. This was, of course, totally in contrast to his previous life when he had been an avowed enemy of the Christian Church. His conversion must have been a great experience for him—a new life, a wholly new relationship to God. But Paul was well aware that he could not live several years later on a spiritual development attached only to what happened back on the Damascus Road.

I'm sure too that we remember another remarkable incident in the experience of Paul when he was given the high privilege of being able to see into heaven with an unusual kind of vision. It was a thrilling experience for him. He speaks of it with a sense of awe and wonder. He did not, however, refer to it often and it is very apparent that, grateful as he was for that inspiration, for that high privilege, he did not base his day-to-day spiritual-growth experience on that which happened once, a long time ago. He did not settle for what happened to him once upon a time as a privileged child of God, and leave it there. So we have in Paul one who recognizes that, grateful as he must be for the blessings that have been his, nevertheless he must "forget the things which are behind" in order that he might not become so attached to them as to be tempted to live tomorrow and the day after tomorrow on just the past—even past glory.

Paul then goes on from there. I am sure that in forgetting the things that are behind, and taking a clean dish, he was very mindful of the fact that it was also his privilege as a redeemed child of God to forget the sins that were behind. Have you ever stopped to wonder what it must have been like for the Apostle Paul to write these letters of the New Testament? The peoples of Corinth and of Philippi were aware of the fact that he had once been the worst enemy of the Christian Church. When Paul was on the way to Damascus that day, it had been for the purpose of throwing professed Christians into jail, to punish them for their avowed allegiance and loyalty to Jesus Christ. Suppose, then, that Paul had dwelt on this, that he had lived with a twenty-four-hour consciousness of what he had been and what he had done. This would surely have limited not only his spiritual growth, but his witness to such a degree that his name would probably not have survived the centuries of the church's history.

Paul was very conscious of the fact that he was a sinner. He said he was probably the worst of all. He referred to all the defeats that had been a part of his life's experience, the time when he had failed his Lord. "O wretched man that I am! who shall deliver me from the body of this death?" he says.

But Paul was aware of something else: he was aware of the grace of God. He was aware that God had shown him undeserved favor, coming to him in the person of Jesus Christ as the Redeemer who had taken upon Himself the burden of all Paul's guilt; that on the cross when He died for the sins of men, He died for every one of Paul's sins. No longer did he stand guilty before God. While Satan may have come to Paul to remind him of past forgiven sins in order to weaken him spiritually, it was not Jesus Christ who did so. Christ had not only forgiven but

He had forgotten, even as the Old Testament reminds us.

There is a little incident that occurred in my early ministry that may illustrate my point here. A fine, elderly lady was living her last days in a hospital bed in Madison, Wisconsin. We chatted together one day about many things. It was evident to me that she was a splendid Christian personality who had lived a rich life and had given a great deal to her children by way of a Christian heritage. But she was disturbed and concerned, not over past sin in general, nor even over that which had transpired recently, but over that of long ago in the early days of her life. I tried then to remind her of some of the promises of God out of Holy Scripture which have to do with the assurance that God forgives the sin of the repentant believer, and that He forgets as well. To help make this clear, I told her of a father who was seated in the living room reading when his little boy came to his side to ask, "Daddy, what are you reading?" The father said, "I'm reading the Bible." The little boy said, "Yes, but that's not a Bible, that's a geography book." The father then said, "I know it is a geography book. But I was reading the Bible and I found something there which made me look up a fact in the geography book. In the Old Testament it says that our sins are separated from us as far as the East is from the West, and dropped into the depths of the sea. I thought about that and decided I would look in the geography book to see just how deep the seas are. Now I find that they are over five miles deep in some places." Geography books may have been revised since to indicate that oceans are much deeper than that, but the father's point was that he found reassurance that his confessed sins were forgiven and separated from him—that far. It was not for him to live in the cemetery of past sins, digging up their "skeletons," looking and re-examining the "bones," for this could only harm him spiritually. He must now live in the assurance of the promises of God concerning forgiveness.

A soft smile came over the face of this fine lady as she lay on her hospital bed. She had found a better understanding of the promises of God.

I wonder if you and I are fully aware of reassured forgiveness each Sunday when we worship. Our liturgical service has a real depth of meaning; there is a progression in the service that has to do with our own spiritual experience. In the early part of the service we plead collectively as well as individually for the mercy and forgiveness of God: "Lord, have mercy upon me." We ask for pardon.

Then we move on to that part of our worship called the "Absolution." The meaning of that word is not always fully understood. It is the declaration of the pastor, not on his own authority but on the basis of Holy Scripture, that repentant, believing sinners are forgiven. Thus, in our normal experience of worship and within our liturgy, we confess our sins; then we hear God's voice as He declares clearly, simply and directly that we are forgiven. It is an exciting thing for a Christian to know the meaning of the Holy Spirit's work within his heart. This is one of the great wonders of the Holy Spirit's work through the Word.

It is strange, then, isn't it, that in our Christian walk we sometimes find it possible to accept the fact of forgiveness in general, yet find it difficult to accept this forgiveness of specific sins? God's promises deal with the specific as well as the general. If you will live in His Word and let God speak to you daily, then you can know what it means to "take a clean dish" when you start each day. You can then "forget the things that are behind" and in the forgetting of them, do some remembering of God's promises. God's grace is sufficient for you. He will make your weakness turn to strength as He lives within you, granting you freedom from these millstones that hang about your neck. He will give you a hope and a radiance of spirit that will bring warmth to your eyes, a lilt to your step and a joy to your heart in a life lived within the framework of His forgiving love and His promised power. Every day by His grace and to His glory, take a clean dish and live life with a sense of anticipation.

Kneel then before the altar of God to receive the body and blood of your Saviour. This gift is given to reassure you of forgiveness, to feed your soul, and to strengthen your sense of a high and holy purpose.

G. RAY JORDAN

BORN KINGSTON, North Carolina, November 11, 1896; A.B., Duke University (Trinity) 1917, *magna cum laude*; B.D., Emory University, 1920; A.M., Yale, 1921; D.D., Duke, 1935; Litt.D., Lincoln Memorial University, 1950. Pastor, College Place Methodist Church, Greensboro, North Carolina; Wesley Memorial Methodist, High Point, North Carolina; Centenary Methodist, Winston-Salem, North Carolina; First Methodist, Charlotte, North Carolina. Professor of Preaching, Candler School of Theology, Emory University, since 1945. Author of seventeen books, contributor to ten more. In wide popular demand as speaker at universities, college churches, and summer assemblies. Active in denomination and member of various learned societies.

What Do You Remember?

And Peter remembered . . . (MATTHEW 26:75).

THE MENTAL LAPSE of Simon Peter accounts for his spiritual collapse. Because he forgot who he was and what he had hoped to become, he failed Christ—and himself. Ignoring the requisites of a disciple of Jesus, he acted as if he were not related to Him in any way. This is dramatically depicted in the scene enacted in the courtyard of the high priest.

Stand, therefore, near this rugged fisherman where you can get a good look. An impulsive, strong, muscular man of the outdoors, he had probably never run from a fight. Now, he finds himself trembling when a young woman looks him in the eye, and he insists that he is not a follower of Jesus. In spite of his denial of discipleship, however, most of us do not feel like condemning him too harshly. For often we have been frightened as we have felt strain and stress which we never anticipated.

But see what Simon Peter *might* have done. If he could have recalled any one of three important incidents in his life, it is likely that he would not have failed. Suppose he could have vividly remembered the exciting day when, busy with his nets at the fishing boat, he heard and happily answered the call of Christ. Do you think he would have considered denying his friendship for Christ? Again, ponder

59

how he would have felt if he had recalled the hour Jesus looked at him with affection, as He quietly said: "Satan hath desired to have you . . . But I have prayed for thee, that thy faith fail not . . ." (Luke 11:31, 32). Surely he would not have collapsed morally and spiritually! Or suppose he could have envisioned Jesus speaking that notable day He expressed such confidence in him, declaring: "On this rock I will build my church." Recalling these thrilling words, Peter would hardly have failed Christ.

It was his lapse of memory that made it easy for Peter to lie, and then add to his cowardice by vehemently swearing, as he insisted that he was in no way related to Christ. But who of us does not understand at least something of this unnecessary collapse of the Big Fisherman? We feel at least part of his anguish when he remembered how he had denied his Master. No wonder he burst into tears! He could not stand the thought of what he had done.

Like this rugged fisherman, we need not fail ourselves, our friends, or our Christ. Certain places, associated with high hours, have the power to provoke clear thinking. Most of us can recall at least a few cities, or sanctuaries, or homes where something dramatic has occurred, strengthening our will for good and influencing our characters for Christlikeness. To return to such a place and stay long enough to meditate on what happened makes it easier to keep in tune with the purposes and plans of God.

Of course, much more than a geographical locality is involved. It is *what* occurred to us that counts. Nevertheless, just to stand, or bow, or kneel once more as we vividly recall the incident, with keen awareness of its drama, becomes a powerful force.

How well Jerry McAuley understood this! He was so

deeply moved by what happened when he accepted the grace of God, enabling him to abandon slavery to drink and to change defeat by evil habits to triumph over them, that once a year he insisted on going back to the cell where he was imprisoned at the time. Expiating for his mistakes, he entered into a new day, learning what the liberty of God could mean. He never wanted to forget where and how it all happened.

So, George Whitefield once wrote: "Whenever I go to Oxford I cannot help running to the spot where Jesus Christ first revealed Himself to me, and gave me the new birth." If you insist that this place is no more sacred than thousands of others, the answer is: *For George Whitefield it was especially significant.* For him there was the association of a high hour with a particular place that brought added meaning to his mind and heart.

Undoubtedly every person can think of some locale where something notable has occurred in his life, having specific significance with respect to his relationship to God. The size of the town, the beauty of the sanctuary, and the various other physical conditions and outward circumstances are all of secondary importance. It is the fact that this is where we saw beauty, met reality, and began to move into a higher appreciation of the Eternal that counts. The experience itself is of supreme importance.

This, of course, is the reason we come to the communion table. We remember an Upper Room. We recall, with ever-deepening appreciation, all that took place on that eventful evening when Christ said: "This is my body which is given for you. . . . This . . . is . . . my blood, which is shed for you" (Luke 22:19, 20).

To that degree that we know how to evaluate places,

we discover the power of philosophy. Quite often, to be sure, our interpretation of life is associated with places which have become sacred for us. Certainly this is true with regard to the Upper Room. We recall the first communion in Jerusalem and the spiritual message which no one of us can hope fully to understand, but which each of us to some degree can grasp—and experience—each time we participate in this sacramental meal.

Like a giant index finger, here is a fact pointing to the vital relationship of the Upper Room, where a few friends of Jesus' gathered with Him in an hour so holy it is never to be forgotten. When we bow at the Lord's Table with reverence that springs from spiritual insight, we gratefully recall that Jesus gave us this service to help us remember what He said, how He lived, and the purpose of His death.

What is even more meaningful, in giving us this memorial which is also a communion of saints, He assures us that God Himself believes in us. This, to be sure, is one of the most daring ventures of belief possible. For we accept Christ's declaration that it is God's purpose to reclaim and redeem us. At the very center of our theology, indeed, is the Christian confidence that we are redeemable, that *we can be saved.*

The fact that all too often we have forgotten this, or ignored its implications, discloses why so frequently we descend far below the spiritual altitudes where we rightfully belong. Indeed, the average man today, as Rabbi Levi A. Olan of Dallas, Texas, has reminded us, "is hollow, confused, without direction or purpose." Although many of us may not confess that this description is accurate, we have little heart to try to prove it is not.

This tragedy of modern man, however, suggests what

remembering the life and death of Christ could mean. For in our best moments we know that this judgment does not have to be final. Indeed, with the same purpose Jesus had when He met with His disciples in the Upper Room, we can receive what our forefathers knew was God's gracious gift. Although the first-century disciples felt they could never adequately express what God had done for them, it was all so real that they hurried from city to city, proclaiming the gospel appealingly and excitedly. As a result, thousands turned to give thanks to God with all their hearts as they found meaning for life.

Some of the less obvious but deeply moving implications of this unusual insight came to a visitor at the National Museum in Cairo one day, as he was gazing at the gold-covered casket of the young King Tutankhamen. "There," he said to himself, "but for the grace of God, lies Moses." He was right. And what saved Moses from the fate of mere eminence, and thus turned his feet into the way of greatness? He remembered who he was, those who had gone before him, his ancestors, and the God to whom all of them belonged.

The same purpose and power are possible for us under any circumstances. Indeed, at the heart of the message of Christianity is the assurance that Jesus' interpretation of life is dependable. It is relevant today and vital for all of us.

Recall the way Olin Stockwell stated this after spending twenty-three months in prison, most of the time in solitary. At the mercy of the Communists in China, strangely enough he was permitted to keep a New Testament. That book, he tells us, plus Divine Grace, plus the sense of humor God had given him were the three things that kept him from going to pieces nervously. Again and again Olin Stockwell read his New Testament. Eagerly he made himself receptive, mentally and spiritually, to the grace of God. His sense of humor was the cushion for many severe tests. During these long months he was recalling the philosophy and theology which point to a God who can lift us out of ourselves, above ourselves, up to a level on which eventually we do live when we find God.

Martin Niemoller discovered the steadying power of this exciting truth when he declared that at long last he was able to realize that his enemies were not God's enemies. In fact, he came to see that those who were enemies of God were not God's enemies. God is the Friend of all people.

All social and personal redemption hinges on this fact. It is possible because God is gracious. To ponder this in the spirit of Christian prayer is to search for life's deep meaning, until the confirmation of it brings us strength for today, whatever the exacting demands may be.

So, later, the intimate friends of Jesus did not merely recall what their Master had taught them; they also thought of other devoted disciples. This memory became another demonstration of the communion of saints. The same fellowship can bring us encouragement and strength now. Constantly the hosts who have been true to God help us to gain a new sense of security—if we permit them. All those who have been true to God because they have experienced His comradeship can support us at this moment, as we ponder the power which was theirs, and seek the Source they discovered. They encourage us to join the world-wide communion of saints.

Thinking of what this might mean, consider the father who, centuries ago, led his son down a hall where the portraits of their ancestors were hanging. Telling his first-born that these men belonged to him and that he belonged

to them, he insisted that he must never fail them! If this
sounds naïve to us, there is one major reason: the spiritual
has turned into the cynical! Those with moral insight and
ethical devotion, however, can still make the words of
Kipling their own:

> Lord God of hosts be with us yet,
> Lest we forget, lest we forget.

We know all too well that those who ignore their blessed
past will hardly have a present that will provoke gratitude
in the future on the part of their descendants. Certainly
only as we remember Christ today can we become confident that He will remember us tomorrow.

Thinking gratefully of Christ—and of those friends of
His who marched bravely forward with Him, with purposes worthy of God's sons—we find strength coming to
our minds and hearts. For the sacramental service is not just
a memorial; it is an experience of spiritual fellowship. Facing
the crises of today, we cultivate the technique and art of
accepting the comfort, the strength, of those who have
been devoted to right, to truth and to love.

So we move with the early disciples and the first-century
Christians from the Upper Room, in Jerusalem, to Damascus, Antioch, Lystra, Derbe—to all those places where the
friends of Jesus proclaimed the gospel as they demonstrated
its power. Consider Rome, where Paul and his fellow Christians suffered so much. Standing in the Colosseum, meditating on what happened there, again we become aware that
the shed blood of Christ brought courage to the martyrs
to shed their own blood. Humbly and reverently we watch
those who sang while they suffered, because they remembered that Christ died on a cross, *for them!*

Ultimately we discover the deepest truth of Christianity as we live with Christ personally. This, of course, is the central purpose of the Lord's Supper. Essentially our worship is for the purpose of our recalling what Christ has done for us, and what He now means to us. Gratefully thinking of Him, we welcome Him to minds, hearts and lives. Jesus made this real reason for the communion quite plain when, in language so simple, so unmistakably clear that it is unforgettable even in the English translation, He quietly said: "This do in remembrance of me."

To the degree that we are aware of Christ now, we gain assurance that He will remember us. He is our Friend, the Person who makes possible the communion of saints, as He urges us to commit ourselves to God. This exciting truth comes with great force in all those social and personal relationships that underscore the vitality of Christian character. This is not sentimentality; it is the spiritual fibre of life itself.

So we learn to live for the King! Not merely for the people around us, who can become kingly, not only for the kingly persons we can become, but for the King of kings. He is always with us—although we do not see Him with our physical eyes. *We now look to Him; we live for Him!*

Reverently meditating, as we steadfastly keep our attention on Christ, we eagerly unite our voices with Joyce Kilmer as he exclaims:

> Lord, Thou didst suffer more for me,
> Than all the hosts of land and sea.
> So, let me render back again
> This millionth of Thy gift. Amen.

GERALD KENNEDY

BORN AUGUST 30, 1907, Benzonia, Michigan; A.B., College of the Pacific, 1929; A.M., Pacific School of Religion, 1931, and B.D., 1932; S.T.M., Hartford Theological Seminary, 1933, and Ph.D., 1934; LL.D., College of Puget Sound; Litt.D., Nebraska Wesleyan; LL.D., Ohio Wesleyan; S.T.D., College of the Pacific; D.D., University of Redlands; D.D., Bucknell. Ordained Methodist minister, 1932; served pastorates in Connecticut, California, Nebraska; elected Bishop of the Methodist Church, 1948; trustee, Pacific School of Religion, College of the Pacific, Southern California School of Theology. Teacher, lecturer, author; president, Council of Bishops of the Methodist Church, 1960-61. Books written by Bishop Kennedy include: *His Word Through Preaching, Have This Mind, The Lion and the Lamb, Heritage and Destiny, With Singleness of Heart, Go Inquire of the Lord, Who Speaks for God, God's Good News, The Christian and His America, The Methodist Way of Life, A Reader's Notebook* (two volumes), *The Parables.*

Too Great To Accept

*Far be it from me before my God that I should do this. Shall
I drink the lifeblood of these men? For at the risk of their lives
they brought it* (I CHRONICLES 11:19, RSV).

*This is my blood of the covenant, which is poured out for
many* (MARK 14:24, RSV).

KING DAVID WAS encamped in the stronghold of Adullam
and had grown weary of the stale water of the storage
tank. In a moment of longing he said, "O that some one
would give me water to drink from the well of Bethlehem
which is by the gate!" Though the Philistines were encamped at that village, three brave men broke through and
brought the king fresh water from the Bethlehem well.
But when David realized they had risked their lives to fulfill his wish, he poured out the water as a sacrfice to God.
"Far be it from me before my God that I should do this,"
he said. "Shall I drink the lifeblood of these men? For at
the risk of their lives they brought it."

The beginning of Christianity was the gift of the
Saviour's life. We must not forget that when we take the
wine and bread at the Lord's Supper, we are celebrating
the offering up of His body and the pouring out of His
blood. The words are repeated: "This is my blood of the
covenant, which is poured out for many." St. Paul summed
it up perfectly when he wrote: "But God shows his

love for us in that while we were yet sinners Christ died
for us" (Romans 5:8, rsv). There was never any assumption by Christians that they were worth dying for, but
only a wonder that they were offered a gift too great to
accept. Like King David, we can only turn to God in
humility and joy that the water of life is brought to us
by One who gave His life for us.

Let us begin by remembering that God finds us first
through *the gift*. Most of our life is receiving. It is more
blessed to give than to receive partly because it is a much
rarer privilege. We receive more than we are ever allowed
to give, and we grow insensitive to the truth that our life
is always out of balance.

God is the great sustainer of life, and the necessities of
living all come to us from His hand. We sometimes talk
about our creativity and our skill in finding new combinations, but all the material is His. When a man begins to
think of the essentials of life, he is standing in the presence
of God. We are children enjoying our Father's protection
and care. When it becomes clear to us in a great moment
of discovery, religious experience is born.

No man can escape the wonder of friendship, unless he
has grown hard with selfishness. We have received encouragement, faith, inspiration from those who walked
beside us and loved us. The society in which we live has
provided schools, roads, protection. It is a startling thing
to realize that men risk their lives to bring us food and provide us with water. All of us are like David, living on the
risks and sacrifices of our brethren, many of whom we have
not seen.

Nothing will change our point of view more than to
begin counting our many blessings. Men wrong us and
people let us down. But we could not live at all if a vast

number of faithful persons did not do their duty and render their service to our welfare. The waves of self-pity which roll over so many of us would recede if only we considered our gifts. When we kneel at the communion altar, we are being confronted with the best gift of all. Here is God giving Himself in Christ; here is the blood of the covenant being poured out for our redemption. Here are symbolized all the wonderful gifts being showered upon us which come only because Jesus Christ lived and died and lived again.

There is an organization which produces concerts for school children. It is called Young Audiences and presents more than 3,000 programs a year by fine musicians. A little girl burst out suddenly during one of the concerts: "Oh, isn't this good! I thought all music came out of a box." And sometimes when we are partaking of the sacrament, it comes to us that our life is not something neatly packaged, but its source is in the One with whom we commune.

Now let us consider *the cost*. Is a drink of water from the Bethlehem well anything to get excited about? It is when it demanded that three men risk their lives for it. Is freedom more than a word? Yes, it is much more than a word and nothing less than the blood of men.

There are many cheap gifts and there is too much costless giving. We are all grateful that the government makes it possible for men to support good causes and receive income tax deductions. This encouragement is generous and right. But we are in danger of making our giving nothing more than a good deal, or a gesture at the expense of the government. Our appeal is not so much to generosity as to business sense. Many a man's giving is done now with one eye on the tax advantage.

Ours is a time of luxury and surplus wealth. We must

stimulate people to want things they do not actually need. Giving becomes a problem for people who must find something novel and useless for the man who has everything. It is a far cry from frontier life when the necessities were sometimes lacking. We have gone a long way from the experience of sharing with each other because everybody was poor and in need of his neighbor's help.

In the summer of 1959, Adlai Stevenson visited John Steinbeck in Somerset, England. The novelist was working on a book about King Arthur and he talked about the simple goodness and heroic struggle of that period. When Steinbeck returned to the wealth and luxury of America in November, he wrote to Stevenson and talked about Christmas. He told of the simple joy and reverence of a child opening his single gift, knowing it meant love and sacrifice from his parents. Then he spoke of gifts piled high, wrappings hastily torn off, and the child saying impatiently: "Is that all?" Listen to these words:

Well, it seems to me that America now is like the second kind of Christmas. Having too many *things* they spend their hours and money on the couch searching for a soul. A strange species we are. We can stand anything God and Nature can throw at us save only plenty. . . . If I wanted to destroy a nation, I would give it too much and I would have it on its knees, miserable, greedy and sick.

It was a great moment when David understood the cost of a cup of fresh water. It would be a good thing if we could remember it when we artlessly turn the tap for a drink. In some communities, water comes from a long way and its delivery demands not only money but human service and in some instances, human life. Health is such a precious possession that if we have a sick day, we know we have no right to complain if health is ours. Yet the cost of health is beyond measure and the skill and devotion of thousands of people are devoted to it. Can any person accept such a priceless gift without counting the cost?

My country is not something to accept with merely a perfunctory nod on the Fourth of July. No nation remains free unless there are those who are serving freedom with their lives. The cost of a civilization is so great that people finally grow weary of paying it, and it is destroyed. The cost of a country's greatness is not to be had at the bargain counter, and when enough people refuse to pay longer, we lose it.

When the woman poured the precious ointment from her alabaster box on Jesus, the disciples were indignant. Why waste it? Why not sell it? But Jesus understood and so often He is the only one who can understand such an act. For He was doing the same thing and He recognized another who gave her most precious possession gladly. We need nothing more just now than a recovery of the sense of what love costs. At the communion service, God is telling us again just how much He loves the world.

Mark Twain sometimes began his lectures by introducing himself as if he were a third person. He would say, "I don't know anything about this man. At least I know only two things; one is, he hasn't been in the penitentiary, and the other is, I don't know why." There are times when any man wonders why he has escaped the penitentiary or worse. Then it comes to him that he has been saved by gifts too costly to measure.

Now we ought to consider further, not only the gift and the cost, but *the acceptance*. David could have taken the water and drunk it carelessly. But his loss would have been terrifying. To take a gift like that thoughtlessly would have marked him as a human failure indeed.

Our danger is in taking the gifts of life and God too easily. Children usually accept the contributions of their parents without much thought. It is assumed that this is their due and these things belong to them as a right. Later on, often when it is too late, the realization comes that one could never pay for what he received from his mother. He could never find the words to express his thanks properly to his father. Every child is given a drink that demands the life of others.

I think that most marriages grow stale when the wonder of the gift is lost and love is accepted as something commonplace. To begin each day with the consciousness that another's life and companionship is yours will keep any marriage in the realm of miracle. One of the most unlovely characteristics of people is their tendency to accept the priceless gifts as a matter course.

If history does nothing else, it ought to remind us of the struggles of good men to create a decent society. Every generation needs to learn anew about the conflicts by which civilization came to it. The sentimental picture of a yesterday that was just old-fashioned styles and slow, relaxed living is soon exploded. Yesterday, like today, was a time of struggle and sacrifice. It was a battle for goodness and a crusade against evil. This freedom was not easily won and I have no right to take it easily. It comes to me as the water came to David, at the risk and often at the price of other men's lives.

When young people begin to understand truly what their parents have given them, it sometimes changes their lives.

Boys are redeemed when it bursts upon them that two people sacrificed their own lives for them. Just a brief glimpse of a woman's quiet love will burn out the pettiness and create some greatness in a man. A partial realization of our national heritage will send a citizen into the arena to do battle for the dignity and rights of free men. But more than all of these experiences, great as they are, is to see the cross. For here is God in Christ, suffering with His children and opening the gates of heaven. The cross is our Lord conquering sin and death. Here is the Messenger bringing us the water of life everlasting and we can only accept it in awe.

On one occasion, when a preacher was marrying a young couple, he put the usual question: "Wilt thou have this man to be thy wedded husband, to live together after God's ordinance in the holy estate of matrimony?" The answer was not the usual shy, soft "I will," but a firm, clear reply: "Yes sir, that's what I came here for." I like that spirit and I wish we might have it when we come to the communion table. Will you accept this gift? Yes, we will accept it with humble thanksgiving, for we came here knowing something of its priceless wonder.

Finally, we are brought face to face with *the debt*. How does a man ever repay men who risk their lives for him? What does one say to a Saviour who pours out His own blood for his salvation?

This being under obligation is an experience we fear and dread. In spite of the fact that most of us are never completely out of debt financially, it is our dream and hope to owe no man one day in the future. This is the heart of our ambition to be independent. What a day that will be, thinks the young man, when I can face the world without debts. For the person who owes another is never quite his own man.

There is a pride in all of us which tempts us to cut ourselves free from obligations to others. The man who looks down on other men says that he stands on his own feet and everyone else should do the same. The man who despises another's weakness points to his own discipline as proof that every man can do likewise. He who secretly suspects he has greatness within, which has not been properly recognized, can never feel superior if he must acknowledge that he is in debt and cannot pay.

Think of David! He was the King and his rise had been spectacular. From an outlaw chief with a price on his head, he had become the ruler of the united kingdom. He was on his way toward a magnificent reign. Did it bother him to acknowledge that everything he had attained or might attain was dependent on other men? Perhaps, but one sure sign of his greatness was that he did not hesitate to acknowledge what he owed.

Actually this sense of debt turns into one of the glories and joys of life. John Newton described it in his hymn:

> 'Twas grace that taught my heart to fear,
> And grace my fears relieved;
> How precious did that grace appear
> The hour I first believed.

There is nothing more uplifting and strengthening than to know that somebody cares for you. Many a man has been saved by the assurance that there was one friend who was deeply and eternally concerned about him. It is when we feel isolated and unrelated that we go wrong. If I can believe that my wife, or my family, or my friends really care what happens to me personally, I find new strength. There is no more wonderful gift for one man to give another than the simple affirmation: I believe in you.

David may have lost his pride but he gained the joy of humility. Three men risked their lives for him! So at the communion service, we lay aside the foolish pretenses of our self-sufficiency and accept His gift which makes us forever debtors.

What can we do about the gift and the debt? We can only do what David did: pour it out unto the Lord. We must do what the disciples did: pour out our lives in His service. So the last word is not sacrifice, or debt, but joyful and triumphant living. Life becomes a pilgrimage with a vision. From the beginning of it, we will have the anticipation expressed by Christian in *Pilgrim's Progress*! "I see myself now at the end of my journey; my toilsome days are ended. I am going now to see that head that was crowned with thorns, and that face that was spit upon for me." What can we do with a gift too great to accept? We can only offer it up to God who gave it to us.

LOUIE DEVOTIE NEWTON

BORN SCREVEN COUNTY, Georgia, April 27, 1892. A.B., Mercer University, 1913; A.M., Columbia University, 1915. Professor of History, Mercer University 1915-1917; YMCA service, Camp Wheeler, Georgia, 1917-1919; editor, *The Christian Index*, 1920-1929. Ordained Baptist minister, 1929; pastor, Druid Hills Baptist Church, Atlanta, Georgia, since April 1, 1929. President, Southern Baptist Convention, 1946-1948. Associate secretary, and a member of Executive Committee, Baptist World Alliance; member, Executive Committees of Southern Baptist Convention and Georgia Baptist Convention. Author, popular column, "Good Morning," in several Georgia newspapers; *Amazing Grace, Fifty Golden Years, Why I Am a Baptist*.

Where Is the Guest Chamber?

The Master saith ... Where is the guestchamber? (LUKE 22:11).

JESUS PLANNED it all—the particular house in which the supper would be served, and the one room in that house, the guest chamber. He does not tell us the name of the owner of the house, though the record in Matthew makes clear the ownership in these words:

"My time is at hand; I will keep the passover at thy house with my disciples," said Jesus (Matthew 26:18).

Mark and Luke declare that the owner would respond to the Master's request for the guest chamber, and when they entered the house, the room was ready and waiting for them. The owner had prepared the guest chamber, but the disciples prepared the supper.

There is a beautiful tradition about guest rooms, dating back to II Kings, when a "great woman of Shunem" said to her husband: "Behold now, I perceive that this [Elisha] is an holy man of God, which passeth by us continually. Let us make a little chamber, I pray thee, on the wall; and let us set for him there a bed, and a table, and a stool, and a candlestick; and it shall be, when he cometh to us, that he shall turn in thither" (4:9, 10).

As long ago as Elisha, and even before Elisha, we have the tradition of the guest chamber, with special thought of God's servants dwelling therein. Down the ages the tradition survived, and many of us give thanks unto God upon every remembrance of the guest chamber, and the blessing of that special room, dedicated to friendship and fellowship. The idea deepened into the thought of maintaining the guest room in one's heart, beautifully expressed by a modern poet, Mary Robinson, in these lines:

> There is a temple in my heart;
> A temple swept and set apart.

Dwelling for a moment longer on this cherished tradition, I recall in my childhood how we joined as children with our parents in preparation of the guest chamber when the beloved old pastor of our little rural church would be coming for the weekend of his monthly preaching engagement. One boy would fill the woodbox by the fireplace in the guest chamber, and carefully set the kindling, ready for the match. Another boy would gather flowers from the yard and woodland—the particular flowers the pastor most admired. Another boy would claim the privilege of blacking his boots.

Jesus knew about guest chambers, where God's servants might rest and pray. He loved folks who kept house for Him—a guest chamber in the home, and a guest chamber in the heart.

And this unnamed friend in Jerusalem had a guest chamber ready for Jesus, happy to make it available when the Son of God declared: "My time is at hand." Do we have a guest chamber in our homes today—in our hearts today—ready and waiting for Jesus?

But let us move on to the meaning and purpose of that particular guest chamber of which Jesus is speaking in our text, and the meaning and purpose of the guest chamber in which we gather about the Lord's Table in our modern meetinghouses. What happened in that guest chamber in Jerusalem?

It was His Table—is His Table, and about His Table, He meets with His own. Let us remember, when we come to the blessed hour of the Lord's Supper, that only the Master has the right to challenge the one who ventures to enter without having on the wedding garment. Paul declares that they eat and drink unworthily who fail to discover the body and blood of Jesus.

Yes, He meets with His own; and He knows His own. Jesus knew that Judas would betray Him, but He allowed Judas to enter the guest chamber, that he might exclude himself. He did not belong to Jesus, and was miserable in His presence. Judas could not remain in the guest chamber, nor can anyone who has not received the Saviour in repentance, through faith.

When Jesus meets with His own about the communion table, He reveals Himself to us in terms of love. Love is the password to the Lord's Table. "We love him because he first loved us. . . . God commendeth his love toward us, in that, while we were yet sinners, Christ died for us. . . . This is my body which is broken for you. . . . This cup is the new testament in my blood, which is shed for you. . . . This do in remembrance of me."

And when He meets with His own about the communion table, we ask, with Isaac Watts:

> While all our hearts and every tongue
>   Join to admire the feast,
> Each of us cries with thankful heart,
>   Lord, why am I a guest?

Why was I made to hear Thy voice
And enter while there's room,
While thousands make a wretched choice,
And rather starve than come?

Let us ask again, what was the meaning and purpose in gathering His own in the guest chamber, before He suffered?

Tired and soiled from the toil of the day, the disciples needed cleansing. The owner of the house had provided the accustomed basin and water and towels for the washing of the feet of the guests; but none of the disciples remembered to offer this humble service. It was because their hearts needed cleansing that their feet went unwashed.

Jesus girded Himself with the towel, and began to wash the feet of the lowly Galileans. And what did He thus reveal to them? That not only their feet, but their hearts needed cleansing—pride and unholy ambition and selfishness needed His cleansing power.

When we gather about the Lord's Table, we need not only His assurance that we are His own, but also His cleansing touch. Hurrying through the hours of the crowded days of the twentieth century, God's people are defiled by the push and shove of the world. We need His cleansing, and we cry out with the psalmist: "Wash me . . . purge me."

Lord Jesus, for this I most humbly entreat;
    I wait, blessed Lord, at Thy crucified feet,
By faith, for my cleansing I see Thy blood flow:
    Now wash me, and I shall be whiter than snow.
                                    —*James Nicholson*

We ask again for the meaning and purpose of the Master's call to the guest chamber in the long ago, and He makes it clear: "Know ye what I have done unto you?" Does not His question point a third lesson?

He knew that the disciples had been quarreling among themselves about first places in His Kingdom, and He knew that with such cancerous thoughts in their hearts, they could not become effective followers.

Thus He chose the guest chamber to teach His disciples the essential truth that when we follow Him, we think not of ourselves, but of others.

Happy the pastor, the church, the denomination that allows Jesus to teach His own the basic lesson of humility, unselfishness and sacrifice; and we learn this lesson best when we are apart with Him, looking at Him, listening to Him.

In my early ministry, a friend said one Saturday afternoon before the Sunday for the Lord's Supper: "I cannot be at the service tomorrow morning. You do not understand, but one of our deacons kept me from getting a promotion, and I cannot sit there and see him serving the Lord's Supper without remembering how he treated me."

Turning to the telephone as soon as the young man left the study, I called the deacon in whose office he worked. The deacon came to the study immediately, and I told him what his employee had said. Surprised and shocked, the deacon asked if I would go with him to see the young man. Within an hour the two men were rejoicing in complete reconciliation. It was easy to unravel the ball, once the deacon explained that he had in his file the letter which urged the young man's promotion, but the home office had decided to send in another young man.

"Pastor," said the young man, "you see now what a great injustice I have done my boss. I ask his forgiveness, and I hope that he will be serving the Lord's Supper tomorrow in the section where I sit."

Jesus went on to say: "If ye know these things, blessed are ye if ye do them." Yes, Jesus teaches His own today, even as He taught the eleven in the long ago in the guest chamber in Jerusalem.

Turning now for one last lesson from the Master as He meets with His own, cleanses His own, teaches His own, let us hear the testimony of Paul as he reports the blessed truth about the Lord's Table. It is that word about His coming again, recorded in I Corinthians: "For as often as ye eat this bread, and drink this cup, ye do shew the Lord's death till he come." Till He come!

The message of hope—Jesus' method of cheering His diciples. We must understand that He must die on the cross, but after Calvary would be Olivet, the prophecy of His return to claim His own! The riven, risen, reigning Lord of Life! "Because I live, ye shall live also."

Yes, Jesus cheers His own. "Let not your hearts be troubled. . . . I go to prepare a place for you. And if I go and prepare a place for you, I will come again, and receive you unto myself." On Calvary He revealed His love; on Olivet He revealed His eternal message of hope; and when we gather with Him in the guest chamber to receive the broken bread and outpoured wine, He certifies His love, His cleansing, His teaching, and His assurance of immortality.

And now one solemn thought: How shall I prepare for the guest chamber? Do not our hearts agree that it is only in reverent worship—in adoration, thanksgiving and confession—that we dare enter His guest chamber?

Amidst us our Beloved stands,
  And bids us view His pierced hands;
Points to His wounded feet and side,
  Blest emblems of the Crucified.

If now with eyes defiled and dim,
  We see the signs, but see not Him,
Oh, may His love the scales displace,
  And bid us see Him face to face.

GORDON POWELL

BORN WARRNAMBOOL, Victoria, Australia, 1911. Educated at Melbourne and Glasgow Universities. Chaplain, R.A.A.F., 1942-1945. Minister, Port Adelaide, 1938-1942; Collins Street Independent Church, Melbourne, 1946-1952; St. Stephen's Presbyterian Church, Sydney, since 1952. Wednesday service attracts the largest midweek congregation in the world and is regularly broadcast and televised. Vice-Chairman for Billy Graham Crusade in Australia. Special preacher, Olympic Games Service, Melbourne; Marble Collegiate Church, New York; New York Avenue Presbyterian Church, Washington; Montreat Conference, North Carolina; City Temple, London. Author of *The Innkeeper of Bethlehem* (1960) and six other books.

Betrayed, He Gave Thanks

The Lord Jesus the same night in which he was betrayed took bread: And when he had given thanks . . . (I CORINTHIANS 11:23, 24).

THIS IS A most surprising statement, surely! Normal people when they are betrayed burst out in bitterness or they panic. They fight back or they despair. They don't sit down to a meal and give thanks.

When J. M. Barrie was betrayed—his wife deserted him for another man—the genius who created the immortal Peter Pan shut himself away from his fellows. For weeks he paced his room night and day in torment of mind and soul. He was unable to think, unable to talk, unable to create.

One day during the Second World War I was sitting in my chaplain's hut in New Guinea when a distraught young airman arrived with a letter in his hand. His wife was asking for a divorce because she wanted to marry the man who had been the airman's best friend back home. He pleaded with me to use my influence to have compassionate leave granted him so that he could return to Australia. "What do you plan to do when you get back?" I asked. With deadly earnestness he replied, "I'm going to shoot them both." For his own sake special leave was not granted and by the time he was able to go home, sanity had returned.

To take another example of the more normal reaction to betrayal, I think of a letter I received not long ago from the wife of a share-farmer. This man had no capital, but he was strong and willing to work. A wealthy landowner put him on some property which had been neglected and was overgrown. The agreement was that the share-farmer was to clear the land, sow a crop and, after the harvest, they would each take half the proceeds. All went according to plan until just before the crop was ready for harvest, after many months of back-breaking work. Then the landowner found a pretext for evicting the share-farmer and his family. They were now in a desperate plight, but friends helped them to fight the case in the courts. Eventually justice was done.

Some people, like this man, fight back when they are betrayed. Others become bitter, others despair. Jesus might have said, "I've given my very best to these people and this is the result. All men are liars and traitors. I give up." Our Lord did not despair. Nor did He fight back. The same night in which He was betrayed He took bread and gave thanks!

Some may say that this is putting too much emphasis on the thanksgiving. It was little more than grace before meat. But in this case it must have been more than that. Matthew, Mark, Luke and Paul all mention the thanksgiving. As the disciples looked back later to that momentous night, three things seemed to stand out: it was the night Jesus was betrayed, it was the night on which He gave thanks, and it was the night on which He instituted the sacrament of Holy Communion.

Apart from the grace before meat, Jesus in the Upper Room offered a long prayer in which thanksgiving took a prominent part, the prayer recorded in the seventeenth chapter of John's Gospel. In this prayer Jesus gave thanks that He had "power over all flesh," that He had "finished the work" which His Father had given Him to do, and that He could say, "All mine are thine and thine are mine." He had lost none of those committed to Him except "the son of perdition." Our Lord's prayer of thankfulness in that dark hour when the world seemed to be crashing round Him deeply impressed the disciples. They never forgot it. In the light of His thanksgiving in that hour let us consider three truths about the spirit of gratitude.

Gratitude prevents us from becoming obsessed with what is wrong. A normal person betrayed as Jesus knew Himself to be that night would have been able to think of nothing else. Allowing his mind to become filled with dark thoughts, he would have made the wrong decisions and done things to worsen, rather than improve, the situation. Not so with our Lord Jesus Christ. He kept His mind strong and clear by giving thanks for all the good that still remained, giving thanks that in spite of Judas and all evil forces, God was still on the throne of the universe.

Every true follower of Jesus will remember to be thankful even in the darkest hours. I think of John Legge Poore, a Congregationalist minister, who a century ago felt the call to leave a thriving church with a thousand members in Manchester, England and to sail for Australia to minister to the scattered settlers there. One day he rode his horse for hours through weather so cold and wet he was unable to light a fire that he might boil a billy for his tea. Wet through and hungry he came to a settler's hut late in the evening. The hut was so small he had to sleep in a tiny addition with nothing between him and the storm outside except a thin sheet of calico. At the end of the day John Legge Poore wrote up his diary and concluded with the words, "My successor will fare better and be thankful, as I am." I feel certain that if Mr. Poore had allowed his mind to become filled with all his difficulties and hardships he would have returned to England within a few months. But because he was convinced that God had a purpose for him in Australia, he rejoiced to serve Him whatever the sacrifice. His devotion and example inspired scores of other ministers to leave the comfort and security of Britain and serve Christ even to the uttermost parts of the earth.

Again I remember an occasion when, after returning from war service, I discovered that an elderly friend of mine was now an inmate of a large hospital for old men. I knew he had no family and when they told me his wife had died and that he had lost his eyesight, I prepared myself for what I thought must be a distressing visit. I entered an enormous ward and was informed my friend was in the bed at the far end. I made my way down the long center aisle. As I did so, pathetic figures called to me. Many of them complained their relatives no longer came to visit them. Others said the food was dreadful, the staff neglected them, the ward was too cold and so on, endlessly. As I neared my friend, who had some real cause for complaint, I grew more and more depressed. It did not help when I found him lying on his side, his face to the wall. Nor did it help when I discovered that not only had he lost his sight, but he had practically lost his hearing as well. Eventually I managed to get through to him. Immediately he sat up and gripping my arm poured forth a paean of praise to God for all His goodness. It was a wonderful thing that

Australia should look after lonely old people like himself, it was a magnificent hospital, the food was marvelous and the nurses were angels. Truly as we give, so we receive. By his spirit of gratitude this wonderful old man kept his mind from becoming obsessed with all the things that were wrong. In this way he kept himself serene and happy and loved to the end. He was a worthy follower of our Lord who on the night in which He was betrayed, gave thanks for all the blessings that yet remained.

Gratitude is a source of strength. Not only does gratitude keep out the dark thoughts which undermine our spiritual, mental and physical resources, but it becomes a channel of extra strength. In this respect I would like to share a personal experience which taught me a most important lesson. In 1956 I was invited to travel the length of New Zealand preaching and lecturing. In that country there is considerable interest in spiritual healing. It so happened that the previous year, because of deteriorated discs in my back as revealed clearly in X-ray photographs, I was advised by a prominent specialist to have a major operation. However, we had two prayer groups in my church in Sydney assisting us in our work of intercession for individuals who were ill. One of these groups, hearing of my distress, held a special season of prayer for me and as a result I felt such relief I gave up the thought of an operation. I did continue with a surgical brace for several months to give the back support, but I was soon able to discard that. In New Zealand I wondered whether the very heavy schedule, the many forms of travel and the different beds night after night might bring on the trouble again. Instead, my back seemed to grow stronger. I wondered why that should be and came to the conviction that there was a direct connection with the fact that daily I was giving my first-hand testimony of this spiritual healing and publicly acknowledging my gratitude to God for it. Jesus, you remember, laid great stress on the gratitude expressed by the tenth leper. From years of experience now in the field of spiritual healing I am convinced that the expression of gratitude to God is an important factor in permanent healing. Apart from the joy of sharing our blessing with others, it is in itself a channel through which strength flows, spiritual, mental and physical.

There is another direction in which gratitude is a source of strength. I refer to the fellowship of the church and the fellowship of the family. In the eleventh chapter of First Corinthians, from which we take our text, Paul has been referring to the unhappy divisions and rivalry existing in the Church at Corinth. To bring them to their senses he reminds them of how the Lord's Supper began. He stresses how it began on the night Jesus was betrayed (the first great tragic division in the church). Having said that, Paul at once reminds them that that night He gave thanks. In particular He gave thanks for the eleven faithful disciples who remained.

If church people would only give thanks for one another and praise God for all the things that are right in the church, there would be far fewer hurt feelings, far less division, rivalry and disloyalty. At least once every month a minister should publicly give thanks to God for the loyal people of his church, for his office-bearers, for his staff, for the members of the choir, the teachers of the Sunday school, the leaders of the various church organizations and for every faithful member. Not only would it help to make people feel they are appreciated and their work is important to the Kingdom of God, but in a way I can't analyze, spiritual strength flows to the whole fellowship of the church when such gratitude is expressed.

The same principle applies to the family. People who take one another for granted build up resentment and deep tensions which can destroy marriages and bring the utmost misery to children. But where there is appreciation and especially where there is family prayer in which together the members give thanks for their united blessings and for one another, then there is built a solidity and a loyalty which almost nothing in this world can break. In such united expression of gratitude strength is given, and undoubtedly the family that prays together stays together.

In that dark hour of His life when Jesus needed all the strength He could muster, He took time to give thanks. Obviously it was something much more than a religious habit acquired in childhood. It was something which the disciples specially noted on that occasion. They realized that through that prayer Jesus gained in strength.

Let us look again at that for which He gave thanks. First it would be simple gratitude for food. It has been well said that when we say grace before meat we cannot do so without thinking for a moment of the amazing providence and goodness of God. Such a thought should steady us and relax us, taking away the strain. Even at the physical level we benefit because then we digest our food better.

At the Passover, Jesus would give thanks for the mighty deliverance vouchsafed their people centuries before when they were brought up out of slavery in Egypt. So would they remember the good hand of their God upon them in those far-off days and down through all the intervening years. Such memories would strengthen mind and spirit.

But again I am sure that Jesus, in terms of His own teaching, gave thanks in advance for answered prayer. He knew that whatever suffering lay ahead that night and through the coming day, the purposes of God could not be frustrated and He would not allow His Holy One to see corruption. He thanked God in anticipation for the finishing of the work He had come to do, though that work was not completed until the following afternoon. He thanked God for a far mightier Passover, the deliverance from sin about to be wrought for mankind. So our Saviour gave thanks, and in giving thanks extra strength was given Him to face the ordeal that was necessary.

Gratitude should be the key-note of our celebration of communion. Communion means many things to many people. For some it is the means whereby they make most vital contact with the living Lord. For others it is essentially an act of remembrance and of loyalty. Each from the reality of his own experience will decide what is the most important element of communion, but we neglect something vital if we forget that from the beginning the service was essentially one of expressing gratitude. The early church called it the Eucharist, a Greek word meaning "thanksgiving." We are told in Acts 2:46, "And they, continuing daily with one accord in the temple, and breaking bread from house to house, did eat their meat with gladness and singleness of heart, Praising God. . . ." Early in the second century, Pliny, in a letter to the Emperor Trajan, described the Christians in his province of Bithynia. He said they rose before dawn to hold their services (of communion) and sang hymns to Christ as God.

Is it any wonder the early Christians were filled with an overwhelming sense of gratitude? To them had been granted the tremendous experience of seeing the empty tomb, the grave-clothes undisturbed, of meeting the risen Christ face to face. "The power of the resurrection" was to them an experience which had changed all their lives. They knew their sin had been dealt with on the cross. Filled with the Holy Spirit they felt "free, right and happy" with the Lord their God. Gladly they celebrated communion to "do this in remembrance" of Him and to give thanks yet again for the unspeakable blessings that were theirs. In the way He had asked it should be done, they poured out their gratitude for His love and sacrifice. Many of them were facing betrayal, all of them were facing danger and persecution, but however dark the day might be, they emulated their Lord, who, in His darkest hour still took bread and said a prayer of gratitude. Whatever our circumstances, let us too at the communion service take bread and give thanks. God grant that we also may find the strength that they found in this service of thanksgiving. As we "do this in remembrance of Him," let us remind ourselves that He found peace and strength when, on the night in which He was betrayed, He took bread and gave thanks.

EDWARD HUGHES PRUDEN

BORN CHASE CITY, Virginia, August 30, 1903; B.A., University
of Richmond, Virginia, 1925; Th.M., Southern Baptist Seminary, Louisville, Kentucky, 1928; Ph.D., University of Edinburgh, Scotland, 1931. Graduate study, Yale Divinity School.
Pastor, First Baptist Church, Petersburg, Virginia, 1930-1935;
guest professor of English, University of Shanghai, China,
1935-1936; pastor, First Baptist Church, Washington, D.C.
since 1936. President: District of Columbia Baptist Convention, 1939; Washington Federation of Churches, 1940; American Baptist Foreign Mission Society, 1945; American Baptist
Convention, 1950. Member: Board of Founders, University of
Shanghai; Executive Committee, Baptist World Alliance;
Washington Office Committee, National Council of Churches.
Editorial associate, *Christian Century Pulpit*. Author of *In-
terpreters Needed*, and numerous contributions to religious
books and journals.

World Communion

ON WORLD COMMUNION SUNDAY one is customarily supposed to stress the strong ties which bind Christians together in spite of their denominational differences; but to be rather frank and somewhat personal, I should like to say that I am not exactly in the mood for doing the customary things, for we are no longer living in the kind of world which gave rise to such customs. It is high time that Christians should realize that they have been actually deluding themselves in assuming a unity which they do not possess, and stop soothing themselves with pious phrases which have little substance in fact. In the hymn "Onward, Christian Soldiers" which we sing so frequently, there is a line, "We are not divided, all one body, we," but in our more honest moments we are compelled to admit that this simply isn't so. We are shamefully divided in America into more than three hundred separate denominational groupings. I would not presume to say what our forefathers should have done in another day, but I am sure that we have no right to perpetuate the multitudinous divisions which they have created. There may have been some justification for what they did *when* they did it, but there is no justification for what we are doing now.

Recent years have witnessed the launching of various earth satellites, and regular jet airline passenger service is now available for a trip around the world. We now know more about outer space than we ever knew before, and England, for instance, is 40 per cent nearer to us in point of time than it was just a few months ago. In such a shrinking world our many religious divisions appear ridiculous. It is bad enough to be divided politically, racially and linguistically, but to be divided religiously is intolerable.

I recognize that the moment anyone speaks a word of encouragement regarding Christian unity there arises the specter of an authoritative, oppressive ecclesiastical organization—a super-church that might take away some of our hard-earned personal and congregational freedom. But there are also dangers in remaining separate, and personally I would rather live dangerously trying to achieve unity than live dangerously in a perpetual state of division. I am thankful for my own denomination's history, and I believe heartily in its basic principles, but I see no conflict between that acknowledgment on the one hand and my perpetual longing to be a vital part of the total Church of Jesus Christ on the other. I have no well-defined nor specific plan for such a union, but I am not at all sure that we need one. When people love each other enough, and really want to be together, they discover ways of achieving that objective.

Recently I heard the New York Philharmonic Orchestra in Constitution Hall under the direction of Leonard Bernstein. As I sat spellbound by that deeply stirring music I could not help but notice that the musicians playing under the direction of this Jewish conductor were men whose backgrounds reach back into Eastern Orthodox Russia, into Lutheran Germany, into Roman Catholic Italy, and into Protestant America. But their differences melted away under the impact of a common love for music and an all-consuming desire to reproduce as faithfully as possible the majestic compositions of Beethoven, Brahms, and Bach. I was also intrigued by one of the compositions they played. It was the Second Symphony of Charles Ives, the New England Congregationalist, who was an outstanding businessman in the field of insurance as well as a recognized and honored composer. This symphony is a kind of musical autobiography. It combines in one symphonic composition strains of music which Ives had heard as a boy in various places in a typical New England community. First of all, you catch the strains of some dance music he had heard on Saturday nights; and then there come forth strains of "Columbia, the Gem of the Ocean," reminiscent of the Fourth of July celebrations he had enjoyed in the little town in which he had lived. Later there are strains of hymns which he had heard in the little community church in which he had worshiped as a boy, such as "When I Survey the Wondrous Cross." And then one hears strains of Stephen Foster, representing the music he had heard around the family piano as his mother and father, with their children, gathered together to sing. Having suggested a wide variety of themes and circumstances, he brings them all together in one tremendous musical experience. Of such a nature is the Church of Jesus Christ—a fellowship that is as diverse as mankind itself, but as united as the music produced by the harmonious notes of a great symphony.

It seemed to me as I listened to the music that three basic principles stood out in unmistakable fashion, and all of them were involved in the unity which the symphony was able to achieve. First of all, *it was necessary for the individual player to make certain sacrifices if the results were to be of a superior quality*. There were, for instance, sacrifices in personal concepts of interpretation. Each musician in the orchestra of a hundred men or more is an authority in his field. He has a personal conviction as to what the interpretation of each composition should be. But each musician must sacrifice his insistence upon his own personal interpretation in order that the whole group, playing together, may follow the interpretation of the leader. There were also sacrifices in matters of identity. The audience did not know the name of a single person in the orchestra, with the exception of the conductor. The cellist, the violinist, those who played the drums and the other instruments, were all outstanding musicians, but we did not know the name of a single one of them. They had lost their identity in a common musical venture. There were also sacrifices in the matter of discipline. They had given up many things that they would have ordinarily enjoyed in order to be a part of a great musical organization. Night and day they had applied their talents, their gifts, their God-given abilities, in order to be accepted and to be given a place in such a group.

The second principle was this—*the total group was required to recognize one central, authoritative personality*. Just suppose that musicians in the string section had gotten together and organized and appointed one of their members as the conductor, saying, "*He* must lead this group and *his* interpretation must be followed." And then suppose that those who were in the wood section had gotten together and organized, and appointed one of their members to engage in a struggle for authority. And suppose that those who played the percussion instruments had done the same thing. There would have been utter confusion and hopeless chaos. Only as the entire group recognized the authority of *one* individual could there be harmony and genuine musical achievement.

And thirdly, *it was obvious that the differences of background and tradition did not diminish the effectiveness of their efforts*—the performance was actually more effective because of these differences, for each person brought to his task certain gifts of insight and national heritage which enriched the whole, and made it all the more moving and unforgettable.

So it must be with the Church of Jesus Christ. We do not have to achieve theological identity, but we do have to believe in the integrity of one another's encounter with God. That is the key to the solution of the whole problem. When we are willing to admit that another man's approach to God is just as valid as our own, and that God is just as willing to receive other Christians and to reveal His truth to them as He is to us, we shall be moving in the direction of genuine spiritual unity. On the basis of that common respect and appreciation, we can become so busy working together at the task of reflecting the spirit of Christ, and serving His cause, that the magnificence of our harmonious cooperative activities will drown out all the discords of divergent background and tradition.

> Join hands then, Brothers of the Faith,
> Whate'er your race may be!—
> Who serves my Father as a son
> Is surely kin to me.
> —*John Oxenham*

JOHN A. REDHEAD, Jr.

BORN CENTERVILLE, MISSISSIPPI, December 31, 1905. A.B., Southwestern University, Memphis, Tennessee; B.D., Th.M., Union Theological Seminary, Richmond, Virginia; D.D., Davidson College. Pastor, Presbyterian Church, Farmville, Virginia, 1930-1933; First Presbyterian Church, Tampa, Florida, 1933-1937; Second Presbyterian Church, Charlotte, North Carolina, 1937-1945; First Presbyterian Church, Greensboro, North Carolina since 1945. Popular television, radio, convention, and college commencement and Religious Emphasis Week speaker. Trustee, Davidson College; Moderator, Synod of North Carolina; active in Presbyterian Church in the U. S. and interdenominational service. Contributor to *American Pulpit* Series, *The Pulpit in the South, Here Is My Method, Sermons on Marriage and Family Life, Notable Sermons from Protestant Pulpits,* and *Theology Today.* Contributing editor, *Presbyterian Outlook.* Author, *Getting to Know God, Learning To Have Faith, Letting God Help You,* and *Putting Your Faith To Work.*

Names of the Sacrament

Do this in remembrance of me (I CORINTHIANS 11:24, RSV).

A COMMUNION SERVICE was being held in a little Methodist church in New Zealand. Among the first group to go forward and kneel at the rail was a native first-generation Christian; but for some reason, before receiving the bread and wine, he rose and returned to his seat. Then, a little later, he took his place again and was given the elements with the others. When he was questioned about it afterwards he told this story: "When I went to the table I did not know whom I should have to kneel beside, when suddenly I saw next to me the man who a few years before slew my father, and whom I then swore to kill. Imagine how I felt when I found him kneeling by my side. A rush of feeling came over me which I could not endure, and then I went back to my seat. But when I got there I saw the Upper Sanctuary and the Great Supper, and I thought I heard a voice saying, 'By this shall all men know that ye are my disciples, if ye love one another.' That overpowered me. I sat down and at once seemed to see another vision of a cross with a man nailed to it; and I heard Him say, 'Father, forgive them, for they know not what they do.' Then I returned to the altar."

A sacrament is "a visible sign of an invisible meaning." Here is an outward event, the eating of bread and wine, which had real significance in human experience. And now we explore its meaning by looking at the names by which it is known.

Take first the name, the Lord's Supper. There are two good reasons why this sacrament is called the Lord's Supper.

First of all, it was instituted by Him. When Jesus met with His friends around the table in the Upper Room, He took a piece of bread and thanked God for it. He recognized even in His daily food the gift of God and He would not eat a meal without giving thanks. Then He broke it and gave it to His men and said, "Take, eat; this is my body which is broken for you." It was a symbol of what was to happen the following day. Then after supper He took a cup and gave it to them and said, in effect, "This cup represents the new basis on which God will deal with you. You are no longer subject to the old arrangement, according to which by obedience to the law you must win for yourself divine approval. This cup stands for the new arrangement, the new covenant, the new agreement. Just as this wine pours from the cup, so am I pouring out my life for you. If only you will believe that, and trust the love that is behind it, you will find forgiveness of sins."

Then He went on to say: "Do this in remembrance of me." So this sacrament is called the Lord's Supper not only because He instituted it, but because it is a memorial to Him. It is a means of remembering. Human nature is prone to forget: "out of sight, out of mind" is only too true. When you come to church, the preacher may or may not by his sermon help you to think of Christ. As I walked into the pulpit of a church in Pittsburgh where I was a guest, I noticed the words carved where only the speaker could see them: "Sirs, we would see Jesus." Every true

minister hears and tries to heed that request, but often he
fails. Yet you cannot sit in church and listen to the words
of the institution and witness the distribution of the elements without being reminded of Another whose memorial
is before you.

For example, a friend tells me he knows a father and
son who are the best of friends. Among their many good
times together one stands out above the rest: it was a trip
they took together. The main event of the trip was a hike
to a particular mountain, where they seemed to reach the
height of a beautiful friendship. After they returned home,
there came a day when things did not run smoothly. The
father rebuked the son and the son spoke sharply in return.
An hour later the air had cleared, and they sat with arms
about each other. "Dad," said the boy, "whenever it starts
to get like that again, let's one of us say, 'The mountain.' "
So it was agreed.

Then a day came when the boy again disappointed his
parents and himself. He was rebuked too sternly and left
the table in tears, going to his room. After a while his father
thought he would go up and see the boy, and on the way
he went through the library. There on a sheet of paper,
penciled in large letters so his father would not miss it,
were just two words, "The mountain." And that did it.
The symbol had restored in a moment all that had been
marred.

In the bread and wine we commemorate another mountain, Mt. Calvary, which stands on the horizon of time as
symbol of restoration to fellowship.

There is a second name by which this ritual is known.
It is called not only the Lord's Supper, but the Eucharist.

We do not use this name often; yet it is a good one, and it comes from a word which means "to give thanks."

As a boy I heartily disliked going to church on Communion Sunday, because the whole service was so sad. On other days "church" was just tiresome, but when communion time came everyone looked as though he had lost his last friend. Yet the word Eucharist reminds us that we are attending not a funeral but a feast. We meet for this service, not on Friday when He went to the cross, but on Sunday when He came back to life; and so we celebrate the crucifixion in the light of the resurrection. The proper mood is more of a victory than defeat. We read that when He took the cup He gave thanks. So do we, with a thanksgiving that sings of sins forgiven and life redeemed.

Several years ago in Edinburgh it was my pleasure to worship in a church known as St. George's West. It happened to be Communion Sunday and I was interested to see that they still use the large cup there. The person next to whom I was sitting passed the cup to me without taking the wine. I naturally wondered why, and then I remembered having read of an incident which occurred in that same church some fifty years ago. One of the assisting ministers was Dr. John Duncan. He was professor of Hebrew at the University, where his students called him "Rabbi" because he very much looked the part. He noticed that a woman sitting near the front passed the cup without drinking the wine, and when he saw her eyes dampen with tears, he walked to the pew and took the cup. As he handed it back to her, he said, "Take it, woman; it's for sinners."

As the meaning of that truth sinks in, you can understand why the Lord's Supper is called also the Eucharist.

The third name by which this sacrament is known is

communion. The word means to partake of something with another; and in this meeting together we commune not alone with each other but with Him.

We call this the Lord's Table. He is Host and we are guests. Sometimes when you wish to show a courtesy to another but cannot be present yourself, you ask a friend to substitute for you and give what you call a proxy luncheon. But this is no proxy affair. Jesus is no absentee host; He is present to commune with His guests.

Christians differ of course as to how this Presence is to be known. Roman Catholics teach a doctrine of transubstantiation, meaning that the bread and wine are changed into the actual body of Christ. As Protestants we believe that the Presence is spiritual, which means that it can be known in those parts of our being which are spirit. Our minds are spirit, and when we find ourselves thinking His thoughts after Him, He is here. Our hearts are spirit, and when we find our feelings cleansed and ourselves loving as He loved, He is here. Our wills are spirit, and when our aims parallel His purpose, He is here.

A woman went to church in New York one day. She had come to the city to get away from her home, where the members of her family were at sixes and sevens. She said that while the minister was speaking of Dr. Wilfred Grenfell and his work in Labrador, it seemed that the man himself faded from view and the presence of Christ was so real she could see Him walking up and down the aisles of the church, stopping to place His hands upon the members of the congregation and saying to them, "Peace be unto you."

If you would like to have something of that experience, close your eyes and think of Him as standing beside *you*.

See the look of calm confidence in His face. Feel the touch
of His hand upon your shoulder. Note the warm friend-
liness in His voice as He speaks and says: "Be still, and
know that I am God. Come unto me and I will give you
rest. My grace is sufficient for you." And when the service
is over and you go home and some member of the family
who could not be there asks, "Who was at church today?"
then you can answer, "Jesus was there; I know because He
spoke to me His word of peace and of pardon and of
power." When that happens, this Supper will be a real
communion.

Finally, this rite of our religion is known not simply as
the Lord's Supper and the Eucharist and the communion,
but as the sacrament. This word suggests a truth also which
can add meaning to its observance. It comes from the Latin
and is a transliteration of the word *sacramentum*. The
sacramentum was the oath of allegiance which the Roman
soldier took. When he was inducted into service he took
his oath, and at various intervals he was called upon to
renew it.

We have the same sort of thing in our Pledge of Allegiance to the flag. When we stand and salute the flag and
repeat these words: "I pledge allegiance to the flag of the
United States of America and to the republic for which it
stands; one nation, under God, indivisible, with liberty and
justice for all," we are observing the original meaning of the
word sacrament: it is an oath of allegiance, and it is renewed
whenever you repeat the pledge.

So it is today. When you became a Christian you took a
pledge: you committed yourself to Christ and promised to
be a worthy member of His Church. And whenever you
"take communion," as we say, you are renewing that agree-

ment. You are saluting the flag of the Kingdom of God and renewing your pledge to be a good soldier. When you eat the bread and drink the wine, you are giving your word of honor once again that you will keep your promises.

Dr. Arthur J. Gossip, of Scotland, says that one day on a battlefield in France he came on the body of a soldier lying still. "Why," he said, "out of all the hundreds one saw, he so impressed me, I do not know. But he was Scottish, and he was young, and he was somebody's dearest; and those dead eyes seemed to look up into mine, and those dead lips to cry out until I heard, 'This is my body broken for you.' And we had a communion service there of a kind, just we three—the dead laddie, the Lord Christ, and my soul; and I swore that because he had died for us, please God, I would be the worthier for that sacrifice."

Commemoration, thanksgiving, communion, commitment: these are the meanings which come to us out of the names of the sacrament.

> He was the Word that spake it,
> He took the bread and brake it,
> And what that Word did make it
> I do believe and take it.

WILL SESSIONS

BORN JACKSON, MISSISSIPPI, July 26, 1905. A.B., University of Arkansas, 1925; M.A., Drake University, 1935; LL.D., Kansas City College of Osteopathy and Surgery, 1952; D.D., Culver-Stockton College, 1953. Chaplain, Army of the United States since 1934; rank: Lieutenant Colonel; service: two and one-half years in Southwest Pacific Area during World War II. Pastor of Wood Memorial Church, Van Buren, and churches at Corydon, Iowa, and Kearney, Nebraska; pastor of Independence Boulevard Christian Church, Kansas City, Missouri since 1946. Active in civic affairs and the work of the Kansas City Council of Churches: chairman of Radio Committee, and Labor-Clergy-Management Committee. Author, *Greater Men and Women of the Bible, The Week of the Cross.* British-American Pulpit Exchange, 1960.

To Have Been There

WHAT AN EXPERIENCE it must have been for those who attended the Last Supper! Thirteen they were, Jesus and The Twelve. They were so sure that they knew one another. After all, they had been together for some three years during which time they had seen Jesus perform some of the more amazing feats of healing that this world has ever known. Add to this the fact that they had walked the rough roads beside Him, had felt the urgency of His mission, and had thrilled to the very person that He had shown Himself to be.

From the time when He had set His face steadfastly toward Jerusalem, they had realized that a climax lay ahead, but they did not realize what its nature was or what its consequences would be. How could they possibly foresee that He would be arrested, tried, sentenced, crucified, and later resurrected? Their thinking was that what they had done before, they would continue doing. What they had experienced had been an itinerant ministry, and their thinking was that they would go right on sharing in its fellowship. The fact that it was the Passover season meant nothing more to them than any other Passover had ever meant. They had no way of knowing that this Jesus whom they loved was to become the "Lamb of God" (John 1:36) who would take away the sin of the world.

When the day of the Sedar came, Jesus arranged for its

111

observance. They did not realize that it would mark their last meal with Him. To them it was only the traditional celebration of the day. In an Upper Room the feast was made ready. Although the house did not belong to Jesus, He became the self-appointed host. There is a story to the effect that while the table was being set, one of the women who was assisting asked, "Where shall we put Jesus that He may be at the head of the table?" And she received the answer, "It will make no difference where you put Him because wherever He is will become the head of the table." Assuredly His was the magnetic personality. Everything that occurred during His years with The Twelve was made meaningful by His presence. Even to this day, the Last Supper—if it be called that—or the communion—if it be called that—has meaning not in terms of its food or its preparation, but in terms of His presence. If the Christ lives in the hearts of those who keep the feast, it does not matter whether its emblems be served on glistening silver or paper plates, whether its wine be in a priceless chalice or a water glass.

It was the custom in those days to recline at meals. The circumstance gives clarification to two things that took place, the feet-washing which surprised the apostles, and the fact that the disciple whom Jesus loved was reclining on His bosom. The Master, taking the role of host and having no servants, rose from the table and laying aside His outer garment, girded Himself with a towel and proceeded to bathe the feet of His apostles. This was a completely new experience for Him and for them. They did not know what to make of this departure from His normal behavior patterns. Peter is said to have remonstrated, "Not my feet, Lord!" Whereupon Jesus insisted that unless his feet were washed, Peter would have no part with Him when he came into His Kingdom. Immediately Peter pleaded that Jesus should wash not only his feet but his head and his hands. Jesus explained that such would not be necessary, and proceeded with His task. When He was finished, He took His place again at the table.

There is a story from the life of Anton Lang who for many years played the part of the *Christus* in the Passion Play at Oberammergau. A reporter is said to have asked him what impressed him most in portraying the Christ, and his answer was: "I have no way of telling you how I come to love those men as I wash their feet."

Just when Jesus took the bread or just when He took the wine, there is no certain way of knowing. Matthew, Mark, and Luke in writing about the Last Supper tell of the Master's speaking of the elements in that order, first the bread and then the wine. Truly it would have been rapturous to have been there, to have seen how it was first done. There are many artists who have given practically their whole lives in trying to capture the strength and the sensitiveness of our Lord's face. Surely there must have been expressions in His eyes, grimaces that furrowed His brow, movements of His hands that gave emphasis to His thought. The Jews are given to making gestures to this day and it is reasonable to believe that Jesus, a Jew of the Jews, would have made use of His hands and His face in expressing Himself.

Then there would have been His voice. Surely there must have been tones in His speech that would convey command, that would cause devils to fear, and that would cause men to obey. It was through His voice that Jesus won the confidence of the woman at the Samaritan well. In calling

Peter and Andrew, He is said to have used but two words, "Follow me." To the lame man at the pool of Bethesda, He spoke, "Take up thy bed and walk." Anybody anywhere could say that to any lame man any time, but when Jesus said it, the lame man found strength flowing into his sinews. He arose, he took up his bed, he went to his house, a man cured after thirty-eight years of being an invalid. Not just any tone of voice could have achieved it; there had to be authority in His saying of the words.

Peter once spoke in high praise of the way that Jesus talked. It was at the instant when there had been some who had turned away from the Master because He had refused a crown. Jesus had said to the apostles, "Will you also go away?" Simon Peter then answered, "Lord, to whom shall we go? You have the words of eternal life" (John 6:68). Depend upon it, there is forever more than enunciation in any communication, there is the *how* the words are spoken, the *when*, the *where*, the *for-what-purpose*, and there is the *force* that is fused into them. All these factors blend in giving art to speech, and the Master knew how to communicate from heart to heart.

Oh, to have been present to witness the breaking of the bread, to have seen the handling of the cup! Each Christian feels that he would have understood the significance of what was in process. Few are very explicit as to what they would have understood. What appears in the text is the fact that the Master took bread and broke it and gave it to His apostles, and said, "Take, eat, this is my body which is broken for you." Today's Christian feels that he would have known just what Jesus meant by that. Those who were there do not seem to have realized that they were sharing in one of history's more precious moments. Jesus picked up a piece of the unleavened bread that had sustained the lives of the house of Israel when they fled Egypt under the leadership of Moses. What the apostles probably expected Him to say would have been to the effect that here was the bread that the women had been told to bake without waiting for the yeast to leaven it. But instead, the Master was directing their thinking into new channels altogether: "This is my body," He was saying. Surely this was not at all the teaching which they had cherished all their lives. This was not Jesus' body at all, it was the ancient unleavened bread of the Passover; but Jesus was still speaking, "Do this in remembrance of me."

So they ate the bread of their fathers but with a new meaning stirring in their hearts. They had thought of the bread in terms of an ancient need; now it became a reminder not of a past event but of a present Person. This bread through the centuries had been regarded as having holy significance; now they were told to realize that its holy meaning was to be associated with their friend Jesus. He was their Redeemer. He was their Saviour.

It was all very stirring. The apostles fairly wondered if something were the matter with the Lord. He had never behaved after this manner before. Could it possibly be that something was wrong? As they looked into His face they saw that His heart was heavy within Him, and as they listened, He murmured, "One of you shall betray me." It was shocking. Men should not say things like that among their friends, but He had spoken it. The text declared that they began one and all to make inquiry, "Lord, is it I?" Possibly this was because they realized, as all thoughtful men realize, that there lay dormant within their natures the capacity for betrayal. Any man, no matter how much he may have loved the Lord then or now, might well ask prayerfully, "Lord, is it I?" It was at this point that the question was put to the disciple whom Jesus loved, who is believed to have been John, to find out who it was who should betray Him. Jesus said, "He that dippeth his hand with me in the dish . . ." (Matthew 26:23), but actually they all ate from the common bowl. It could have meant any of them. John 13:26 (RSV) records, "It is he to whom I shall give this morsel when I have dipped it." So when He had dipped the morsel, He gave it to Judas. That would seem clear enough, but the meaning of what betrayal involved was lost upon the apostles on that strange and amazing night.

It would have been wonderful to have heard Him say, as He took the cup of wine, "This is my blood." How surely they were bewildered. The rabbi was supposed to explain that the wine had sustained life for ancient Israel during those fearful days when they wandered in the desert. Water could never be depended upon. Only too frequently it was contaminated, but wine could be counted upon, could be poured into the water and thus the water made potable. That Jesus should associate the wine with His blood was new to Jewish ears. No one, however, said one word against what was happening. They listened as men transfixed. "Do this in remembrance of me." Thus, before their very eyes, they saw and they heard the Master appropriate their most ancient symbols of bread and wine, giving to them new meaning, giving to them associations that were personal, and that were unforgettable.

To have been there would have offered its compensations. Too much has been made of the cup. Was it the chalice of Antioch? Was it any chalice? Was it a grail, holy or unholy? Really, the very contemplation of Christendom over the things that Jesus may have touched, or the places where He may have walked, has become so emphasized through the centuries that the substance of what Jesus said, of what He did, and of who He was, has been all but put into secondary consideration. "Remember Me," was the plea that Jesus made.

And Paul has stated the circumstance of the communion unforgettably, "Let a man examine himself, and so eat of the bread and drink of the cup" (I Corinthians 11:28). No one should compel him to commune, no one should separate him from the love of Christ. For each man, the only question that should ever come into his heart is the searching one, "Do I love Thee, Lord?"

None is worthy. None has ever attained the mark of the high calling in Christ Jesus, but surely no greater love has mankind ever known than that which our Lord has shown.

In a world of chaos, in a season of fear and global tension, it behooves those who love the Lord to love Him with a mighty devotion. As each communes, each will have to make clear within his own heart and mind the meaning of the broken body and the shed blood; he will have to ask himself, "What does this mean to me?"

To those who can say, "I am not worthy, but I love Thee, Lord," must come the realization that they must feed not only upon the elements of the communion, but upon the deeper meaning of the teaching of this Son of Man, this Son of God, this Jesus Christ, our Lord.

FREDERICK B. SPEAKMAN

BORN CHANDLER, OKLAHOMA; student, College of Emporia; A.B.,
Phi Beta Kappa, University of Oklahoma, 1940; M.A., Harvard,
1942; Th.B., Princeton Theological Seminary, 1945; Th.D.,
Princeton, 1946; D.D., Washington and Jefferson, 1950. Pastor,
Central Brick Presbyterian Church, East Orange, New Jersey,
and Third Presbyterian Church, Pittsburgh, Pennsylvania.
Teaching Fellow, Princeton Theological Seminary; acting
dean of the Chapel, Chatham College; sometime chapel
preacher at such colleges as Wellesley, Wilson, Chatham,
Washington and Jefferson, Oklahoma University, The Univer-
sity of Minnesota, and Harvard University; guest professor of
Homiletics, Pittsburgh Theological Seminary. Author, *The
Salty Tang* and *Love Is Something You Do.*

Look! The Lamb of God!

I RAN ACROSS a note on it again the other day. You may
have heard it quoted as often as I've had occasion to think
about it, but it never fails to blow a trumpet to my slouch-
ing awareness. It's the haunting incident of that day in a
Paris Cathedral when H. Wheeler Robinson tells of slipping
in to stand near the back of the Church. The great choir
was singing that twenty-third portion of the Mass:

"Agnus Dei, qui tollis peccata mundi, miserere nobis!"

"Lamb of God, who takest away the sin of the world,
have mercy upon us!"

And Wheeler Robinson noticed that a man standing beside him was twisting his hat in his hands like a rag, and
suddenly he muttered audibly, "O, God! O God, what a
dream! If only He could! If only He could!" And with
that the man turned and ran from the Church. Whoever
that man was, whatever his trouble, whatever had brought
him there to the edge of the crowd in a church, then drove
him away in his sudden refusal any longer to be tempted by
something he felt was too good to be true—perhaps it takes
some attempt to glance through that tortured skeptic's mind
to remind us just what is claimed, just what is offered wherever the Lord's Supper is celebrated today, wherever it will
be allowed world over, and in many a place where it is not
supposed to be allowed.

In more kinds of churches than we've time to list, low

119

church, high church, free land, scourged land, cathedral, missionary's hut, chaplain's tent, or under skies such as ours where it's so easy to participate that many who would complain the loudest were the right to it taken from them, will simply not bother. The reminder is seldom far from me at communion these days of a church in Prague where a clergyman I know will be required to file copies of his communion service in triplicate with the authorities. And the Czech police will be at the door to note the names of all who come to communion, to give them no chance to forget that by their very presence they are the watched, the suspected. But they will come!

The Lord's Supper in this year of our Lord! What will it be saying in all the tongues and accents of mankind wherever you'll find it today? That strange, ancient cry, *Behold the Lamb that was slain! Look, the Lamb of God who takes away the sins of the world!* What a dream, the man said, as the twisted hat in his hands cried his own yearning louder than his words. And what a dream it has been, and the thousands of years of the human story have not been able to brainwash it from us, not since the day men in their caves first carved their hopes on stone or painted their longings on the walls with crude brushes drenched with ancient dyes. Always this dream, that, as Carlyle Marney puts it, somehow, somewhere, sometime One will come who can take our sin away. Someone will come who is good enough, great enough, clean enough to free us from what we keep doing to others and keep making of ourselves. Someone will mean for us pardon, forgiveness, release, power to defeat sin.

You can write the human story around that longing. You cannot tell the human story honestly and ignore either that

longing or the guilty certainty that goes with it that whoever is to save us must be hurt! There must be sacrifice!
The Greeks knew that and told a thousand tragic myths
about it. The Persians knew it as they struggled to find
the Son of Light. Rome at its best knew it, and shuddered
to its own death as that great Empire looked to every com-
bination of religion for some ritual, some blood bath, some
sacrifice to release them from their unexplainable sense of
wrong. The strange men knew it who sat on the old circle
stones which still show on some ancient slopes of England,
trying to decide which of them must die to cleanse the
others.

But why that, of all things? Why that terrible certainty
which has made man's religion a butchery as often as it
has been a blessing? Why should that hideous notion of
necessary sacrifice taint the dream of a Saviour? Because
this too we've always known, however dimly—and it has
been dangerous knowledge, for misused it will build an
Aztec temple from ten thousand human skulls, or spur unspeakable voodoo rites in the jungle, or send the flagellants
stumbling along some street in Mexico, hacking and pulping
their own naked bodies with whips and chains—but this
we have always known, *that it is when the good suffers in
love for others that the others are in some way cleansed,
helped, in some way redeemed.*

Look, I don't like for that to be true. I don't want that
to be true, and neither do you. If you and I had invented
life knowing no more than we now know, we'd surely have
put it together in some other way, so that this strange rule
need not hold true, that it is when the good suffers in love
for others it has the power to save others. But we can't too
often remind ourselves, you and I did not invent life.

So the tiny nation of ancient Israel, pygmy little country among the greats of the world, unequal to the task of carrying the terrible burden of knowing more about God than mortals can live up to, Israel cried down the long halls of the centuries her supreme vision through her greatest voice, that of Isaiah, who knew how it had it be, who knew what it would take. One must come who would be "despised and rejected of men, a man of sorrows and acquainted with grief." It will take such a One to bear our griefs and carry our sorrows. For His wounds will be for our trangressions. His bruises will be for our iniquities. It is the chastisement of our peace will be upon Him, that with His scars we may be healed!

That's the dream in its clearest focus. But does that help? Who's going to be able to measure up to that? Who can fill that order? Who will be good enough, strong enough? Who can love enough? In what man born of woman can truth ever so take flesh as to earn the right to walk down our street, knock on our door and say to us, "Thy sins be forgiven thee?" Who must so suffer in love that we can be clean? *Why not God Himself?* If it has to be then who else could it be but God Himself? What ancient faith with all its fears had hinted at but never quite dared imagine. What even Israel could never quite bring itself to name. What modern man, so impatient of the mysteries beyond our reckoning which have created us and sustained us, what we try to avoid even thinking about. *Who could be the Lamb that was slain but somehow God Himself?*

"And when they were come to Golgotha, which is to say, the place of a skull, there they crucified him." He, who the night before, as He sat at meat with His friends, had said, "I have so longed to eat this meal with you. You've known Me, so now you know God. All men will know that you know Me by the way you love. In this world you will have trouble, but courage, lads! I've won! I've out-maneuvered the world by what I go to do for you." Look, the Lamb of God! Look at the bread He breaks and the wine He pours!

We don't know how or why—the Christian Church has never claimed to know how or why what Christ can do for us by way of forgiveness seems to show a plainer face at this service of communion than in any other act of worship. We've just discovered across the years that this is or should be so. And here before the Trophies of Christ's sacrifice for us, we know it's still quite possible not to accept for ourselves the Christian faith's supreme claim and offer. But it takes some deliberate evasion on our part not to be fairly clear as to exactly what that claim and offer is—that it will not be a King you and I need, not at the last. There is a glory to life we grow taller by bowing down before, but that isn't enough. And it isn't just a Judge we need, not in the deep places of our hearts where all our tomorrows are born. There is a Judge, but if the only God there is turns out to be only a Judge, we won't make it. What we need is a Saviour! What we must have is a Love-Come-Alive to free us from all our corrosive guilts. He offers no less than that. He claims to be none other than the One who alone can offer that. "This is My body, broken for you. This cup is the New Agreement in My blood. Drink ye all of it."